PUBLICATIONS OF THE
Duke University Commonwealth-Studies Center

The British Commonwealth

THE LECTURE SERIES

THE BIRTH of the modern Commonwealth of Nations in the midst of the revolutionary era of two world wars of the twentieth century is one of the vital movements of contemporary history which, perhaps because of its orderly and evolutionary development, has not received in the United States the attention it deserves as an important subject for study. Responding to this need for basic research on and understanding of the Commonwealth, the Carnegie Corporation has provided financial assistance for a Commonwealth-Studies Center at Duke University.

The Center is devoted to the encouragement of research by Duke University professors and graduate students interested in the Commonwealth, and to the encouragement of research at Duke University by professors and graduate students from the United Kingdom, Canada, Australia, New Zealand, and South Africa on economic, political, and historical problems. These purposes of the Center are implemented through a variety of specific activities.

1. *Commonwealth Professors at Duke University.* Distinguished scholars and professors from the Common-

wealth are invited to Duke University for varying periods
of time as visiting members of the faculty.   Professor
Kenneth C. Wheare, of Oxford University, served as
Visiting Professor of Political Science during the spring
semester, 1956.   Professor Walter R. Crocker, formerly
of the Australian National University, Canberra, and
more recently Australian Ambassador to Indonesia, will
serve as Visiting Professor of Commonwealth History
during the spring semester, 1957.

   2. *Duke University Graduate Students*.   Advanced
graduate students from Duke University are assisted in
the completion of the field research on their Ph.D. dis-
sertations dealing with Commonwealth affairs.

   3. *Commonwealth Graduate Students*.   A select number of advanced graduate students from the Commonwealth, chosen on the recommendation of selection com-
mittees within the Commonwealth itself, are being assisted
to pursue research at Duke University toward the Ph.D.
degree.

   4. *Duke University Faculty Members*.   Financial
assistance is provided for members of the Duke University faculty whose research requires field work in the
Commonwealth or special work on Commonwealth materials.

   5. *Visiting Lecturers*.   Finally, the Center presents at
intervals series of public lectures by distinguished social
scientists and officials from the Commonwealth designed
to give in broad scope the results of wide and mature
research on and interpretation of the Commonwealth.
These lectures, the first of which are contained in this
volume, will be published from time to time in order
that these thoughtful contributions may reach a wide
student and general audience.   It is anticipated that a

Monographic Series will be added in time to the publications of the Center.

Among the visitors to the Center during 1955, the following delivered single lectures to professional groups or participated in special conferences: Dr. A. Campbell, British Colonial Attaché, Washington; Sir Douglas Copland, Australian High Commissioner of Canada (reprints of this lecture have been distributed by the Commonwealth Studies Center); Professor A. E. Duncan-Jones, Professor of Philosophy, University of Birmingham; Professor W. G. Friedmann, School of Law, University of Toronto; Dr. George Glazebrook, Canadian Minister to the United States; Professor John H. Habbakuk, Professor of Economics, Cambridge University; Dr. Hugh Keenleyside, Director-General, Technical Assistance Administration, The United Nations; Mr. R. A. McKay, Associate Undersecretary of External Affairs of Canada; Dean Kenneth Shatwell, Dean of the School of Law, University of Sydney.

Since the Center is concerned exclusively with the encouragement of research, specific theories or interpretations of Commonwealth affairs appearing in these publications are not an expression of the views of the Center; the authors of the several publications are responsible for the conclusions expressed in them.

The Duke University
Commonwealth-Studies Committee

CALVIN B. HOOVER
J. J. SPENGLER
R. R. WILSON
PAUL H. CLYDE
R. TAYLOR COLE, *Chairman*

The British Commonwealth

AN EXPERIMENT IN CO-OPERATION

AMONG NATIONS

Frank H. Underhill

PUBLISHED FOR THE

Duke University Commonwealth-Studies Center

BY

DUKE UNIVERSITY PRESS

DURHAM, N. C., 1956

PRINTED IN THE UNITED STATES OF AMERICA
BY THE SEEMAN PRINTERY, INC., DURHAM, N. C.

TO

Hugh L. Keenleyside

FOREWORD

THE COMMONWEALTH of Nations, of which Great Britain is the senior member, affords many facets for fruitful study. It is an association of independent states held together by similar interests and common traditions. The leading statesmen of the several states meet together occasionally for consultation without the impetus of solemn engagements and with little likelihood that agreements or enactments will result having any enforcing sanction. Thus the Commonwealth is a unique experiment in international co-operation, which ought to interest all who are concerned with one of the major political tasks of this age.

Each of the members of the Commonwealth has inherited in some degree a share in the institutions and traditions that took their rise and were largely shaped in Great Britain. Each has its own peculiar environment and separate history, which have contributed to make it a unique community having characteristics of its own. Thus the several national histories of the members of the Commonwealth and the institutions evolved in each of the states afford many interesting subjects worthy of study and suggest profitable food for thought. Consequently, the planned interchange of personnel, whether of more mature scholars and teachers or of students at an earlier stage in their careers, promises benefits to those who participate in the interchange and should help toward a better understanding of the general subjects studied.

It was highly desirable, in the outset of this enterprise, to have an authoritative statement concerning some of the more important factors influencing the general history of the Commonwealth and concerning some of the immediate questions suggested by the changing circumstances of the present. To provide this statement, the Committee entrusted with the management of the Center was fortunate in enlisting the co-operation of Professor Frank H. Underhill, who gave in the autumn of 1955 the three lectures here published in substance.

Professor Underhill is a native of Stouffville, Ontario; he was educated in schools in that Province, at the University of Toronto, and at Oxford. He has served as Professor of History at the Universities of Saskatchewan and of Toronto. He is a Fellow of the Royal Society of Canada and has

served as president of the Canadian Historical
Association.   His published contributions to the
history of Canada and of the Commonwealth are
numerous.   He is currently Curator of Laurier
House, Ottawa.

The lectures in this volume will afford to under-
graduates and to other readers a brief, stimulating
introduction to the general history of the rise of
the Commonwealth.   Those who wish more exten-
sive treatments of other phases of the subject will
find intelligent guidance in the appended list of
readings.

W. T. LAPRADE
Emeritus Professor of History
Duke University

INTRODUCTORY STATEMENT

I THANK DUKE UNIVERSITY and the committee in charge of its Commonwealth-Studies Center for inviting me to deliver these lectures on the British Commonwealth of Nations. It is a matter of considerable pride to me that, in launching its program of Commonwealth studies, the Center should have invited a Canadian to give these initial general talks. Canadians are accustomed to think that their country has played a major part in the long, peaceful evolution through the nineteenth and twentieth centuries which has turned the British Empire into the British Commonwealth. Sometimes, in our more boastful moments, we assert that she has played the major part. The historic Canadian achievement has been the preservation of the northern half of North America from absorption into the United States. Apart from this achievement, or as a part of it, we are accustomed to think that the Canadian contribution to the

growth of the British Commonwealth will provide our chief claim for admission into Paradise
when the last trump sounds.

The Commonwealth consists of eight nation-
states: the United Kingdom of Great Britain and
Northern Ireland, Canada, Australia, New Zealand, South Africa, India, Pakistan, and Ceylon.
These enjoy the position of "members" of the
Commonwealth, and each reached the status of
membership by its own peculiar path. To deal
with their individual stories and with the history
of their inter-relations is a complicated task in
itself. But this history, to be fully intelligible,
cannot be isolated from that of a great variety of
other communities. Some of these are now outside
the British connection: Ireland, Burma, Egypt,
Israel, Irak. Others, dependencies of the United
Kingdom, are on their way upward at different
stages, and by processes sometimes not quite peaceful, towards the status of member of the Commonwealth or towards independence outside the Commonwealth. Each of them presents a fascinating
study in itself.

I mention only those that have been much in
the news recently: Cyprus, Malta, Nigeria, the
Gold Coast, Kenya, the Central African Federa-
tion of Northern and Southern Rhodesia and
Nyasaland, Malaya, British Guiana, the British
West Indies. Altogether, there are some forty-

odd of these British dependencies, practically all of them officially dedicated to the proposition that it is possible for them eventually by gradual evolution to reach the status of Canada and India, i.e., to become full "members" of the Commonwealth. They are, most of them, at the same time going through a fever of anticolonialism and are combining a political revolution with far-reaching social transformations. If the British thesis can be demonstrated in all or most of them, that the essence of British colonialism is that it is a preparation for full democratic self-government, a thesis which has been demonstrated in the cases of Canada and the more mature members of the Commonwealth, then surely we have here a very significant subject for study.

In addition, there is another subject of study. Since the modern Commonwealth came to birth in the midst of the revolutionary era of the two great world wars of the twentieth century, no treatment of it would be adequate which neglected its external relations with the rest of the world. A great deal of Commonwealth history in the last generation turns on the relationship of the British countries to the League of Nations and the United Nations, to Western Europe, to the U.S.S.R. and the Communist bloc.

It is also evident that the affairs of the various individual British communities and of all

of them together are getting more and more
"mixed up" with those of the United States. This
new intimate, if not as yet affectionate, relationship which is developing between the British peoples and the American people is the most remarkable of all the changes in the Commonwealth now
taking place before our eyes. The United States
is reaching what Irish republicans would have
called in the 1920's the status of "external association" with the British Commonwealth. To
describe this as the return of the American prodigal
son to his British father's household would invite
loud and indignant denials from every American
citizen; on the British side, one must say, there
is no sign of anyone's preparing the fatted calf
to celebrate the prodigal's return. Nor is it quite
correct to describe what is going on by a good
American metaphor and say that the Americans
are "muscling in" on what were once regarded
as exclusively British imperial enterprises. There
never were such reluctant imperialists as the
American governments of the 1940's and 1950's.
Nevertheless, we are confronted by the undeniable
fact that something new has been added in our
day to the British Commonwealth, something
American. All roads in the Commonwealth lead
to Washington.

To deal adequately with this complex network
of topics is obviously an impossible task in a brief

treatment. The enormous mass of writing about the British Empire and Commonwealth and about its individual states, which now fills our library shelves, cannot be satisfactorily distilled into three essays. A summary chronicle of the main events in Empire-Commonwealth history would be of little use. It is also useless to try to say over again in briefer compass what has recently been so well said about the twentieth-century Commonwealth in the books of such writers as Hancock, Mansergh, Wheare, and Brady, books that are already classics—though one cannot avoid many of the grand old fortifying commonplaces about the British liberal Empire-Commonwealth found in the standard books; the first two lectures are full of them. My purpose has been to concentrate on aspects of the theme of the Commonwealth which seem to me to be of special interest, even though this procedure is apt to lead to a somewhat subjective and perhaps distorted presentation of the subject. Since I am a Canadian, most of the illustrations will be from Canadian history; no doubt this will tend to produce further distortion of the picture.

The first lecture deals chiefly with the nineteenth-century Victorian liberal Empire, which, in the twentieth century, was to transform itself into the Commonwealth. The selected points emphasize its liberal character; some of the darker and uglier aspects of its history are neglected. Liberalism is emphasized, since liberalism is something that we in the twentieth century are finding it more and more difficult to understand; or perhaps one should rather say that, if we think of ourselves as liberal, we are finding it more and more difficult to admit that anybody else is.

The second lecture goes on through the period of the First World War and of the long armistice of the 1920's and 1930's. Books on British imperial history are accustomed to refer to the nineteenth-century Empire as the Second Empire, which grew up after the disruption of the First in 1783. During the 1920's there was some tendency to speak of a Third Empire, which had emerged out of the war of 1914.[1] We can now refer to it more properly as the First Commonwealth:[2] the Commonwealth of Canada, Australia, New Zealand, South Africa, Newfoundland, the Irish Free State: communities which had a long historical association with Britain, which were settled mainly by white people of British stock, which had a long experience in managing their communal affairs through British political and

1. For example, Alfred E. Zimmern, *The Third British Empire* (London, 1926).

2. Lionel Gelber, "The Commonwealth and World Order" (*Virginia Quarterly Review*, Winter, 1954). In this article Mr. Gelber uses the titles "First Commonwealth" and "Second Commonwealth"; he gives a brilliant analysis of the problems involved in the evolution from the First to the Second.

legal institutions and in living together with each other in a freely accepted co-operative association.

The third lecture deals with the Second Commonwealth, which is, in the second half of the twentieth century, emerging out of the Second World War. It already includes three Asiatic, nonwhite communities: India, Pakistan, and Ceylon, which have behind them a long non-British civilization of their own. It seems likely to include in due course other Asiatic and African communities, all peopled primarily by non-British stock. In deference to their susceptibilities there is already a tendency to drop the adjective 'British' from the title of the Commonwealth, thereby suggesting the more insistently that this remarkable multi-racial association, *the* Commonwealth, with its loose free-and-easy form of international association and its abhorrence of definite constitutional structure, is a model which other less advanced, less blessed, peoples might well consider following. No doubt, as many will have observed, when any spokesman from a British country begins to talk about the Commonwealth, he soon reveals an inarticulate major premise underlying all his argument; to wit, that when God is decreeing to begin some new and great period in his Church, He reveals himself, as his manner is, *first* to his Britishers.

I have done my best throughout to avoid this major premise, now made articulate. The most

realistic defense of this liberal Empire-Commonwealth was that offered by John Stuart Mill in
1861 in his treatise on *Representative Government*. In his younger days, Mill had been one
of the most effective propagandists for Lord Durham's Report; in his middle age in the 1860's, in
spite of the predominance of Little England views
among his liberal contemporaries, he continued to
believe, like Durham, that the Empire might be a
permanent, not merely a transitory, phenomenon.

But though Great Britain could do perfectly well without
her Colonies [he wrote] and though on every principle
of morality and justice she ought to consent to their
separation, should the time ever come when, after full
trial of the best form of union, they deliberately desire
to be dissevered—there are strong reasons for maintaining the present slight bond of connection, so long as not
disagreeable to the feelings of either party. It is a step,
as far as it goes, towards universal peace and general
friendly co-operation among nations. It renders war
impossible among a large number of otherwise independent
communities. . . . It at least keeps the markets of the
different countries open to one another. . . . And in the
case of the British possessions it has the advantage, specially
valuable at the present time, of adding to the moral influence, and weight in the councils of the world, of the
Power which, of all in existence, best understands
liberty. . . .

As the last sentence shows, even so stern a
rationalist as John Stuart Mill could not help, now
and then, admiring his own country; but he did
not indulge in a prolonged gush of mystical senti-

ment about its mission in history. I have tried to follow his good utilitarian example.

CONTENTS

The British Commonwealth

The Liberal
Victorian Empire

LIKE SO MANY other practical gadgets for making life on this planet more efficient and more comfortable, the British Commonwealth was invented in America. The idea of the British Empire as being in its essential nature a group of states "equal in status, in no way subordinate one to another in any aspect of their domestic or external affairs, though united by a common allegiance to the Crown, and freely associated as members of the British Commonwealth of Nations" was first conceived by some of the more statesmanlike American colonists round about 1774. The phraseology quoted is from the famous Balfour definition of 1926, but it expresses almost exactly what these Americans of the eighteenth century had in mind. They were trying to find a way by which the union of the colonies with the mother country could continue on a basis acceptable on each side of the Atlantic, in particular on a basis

that would guarantee to the colonists their un-
alienable rights to life, liberty, and the pursuit of
happiness. They reached the conclusion that the
liberty they sought could be maintained within the
Empire only if the colonies were constitutionally
equal in status to the mother country. I need not
burden you with quotations from John Adams,
James Wilson, Thomas Jefferson, or others;[1] perhaps it is worth recalling here that one of these
American inventors was James Iredell, of North
Carolina.[2] They had not time to work out their
new idea very fully, and their theory ran into
great practical difficulties when they approached

1. Samuel Eliot Morison, ed., *Sources and Documents Illustrat-
ing the American Revolution* (Oxford, 1923); Randolph Green-
field Adams, *Political Ideas of the American Revolution* (Durham, 1922).

2. Griffith John McRee, *Life and Correspondence of James
Iredell* (2 vols.; New York, 1857), I, 218-219. In September,
1774, Iredell issued a pamphlet, *To the Inhabitants of Great
Britain*. Answering the argument that, since the Empire consists
of many states, "these states must be subordinate to some power
that shall superintend and regulate the whole," and that, therefore, "the British Parliament residing in the original kingdom
must be possessed of this sovereign authority," and that the legislatures of the American colonies could not set up an *imperium in
imperio*, he replied that the Empire consisted of "several distinct
and independent legislatures, each engaged within a separate scale
and employed about different objects." He went on: "The
principal inconvenience attending our situation we readily admit;
that it may not be always practicable to bring so many different
legislatures to concur heartily in the prosecution and support of
one common object. Judging of the future by the past, I do not
think this would be found in practice so difficult as in speculation
it may appear, but surely any remedy for the evil ought to be
conducted on the basis of a general negotiation, and not violently
sought by an unjust usurpation of power."

the thorny topic of the regulation of trade.   It seems obvious, also, that the monarchy of George III, claiming all the powers of control over policy which he claimed, would not have been found acceptable for long to the Americans even if the British Parliament had been willing to abdicate its sovereignty over them.

Unfortunately, this creative idea of the equality of the legislatures and people of Massachusetts, Pennsylvania, Virginia, North Carolina, with the Parliament and people of Great Britain found hardly anyone on the British side of the Atlantic who could grasp it.   And the Americans who grasped it began to propound it at too late a stage in the controversy, only a few months before the embattled farmers at Concord bridge fired the shot heard round the world. The dispute as to the relative powers and rights of colonies and mother country was ended by the colonies separating from the British Empire and becoming independent.   Thereafter, the American people, their attention concentrated on the new task of building up a continental nation, forgot all about this American contribution to the political philosophy of an Empire that included a variety of communities spread across the oceans.   It was forgotten among the British peoples also.   When the idea of a Commonwealth of Nations was once again propounded and put into practical effect by Jan Christiaan Smuts and Robert

Laird Borden and their contemporaries in the years 1917-1919, nobody at first remembered that there were American precedents in 1774. Nobody even remembered that the word *commonwealth*, with its connotations of government based on consent and the equal participation of all citizens in the making of communal decisions, had been a favorite term with the American colonists.

But it was not altogether accidental that, at the same moment at the end of World War I in 1917-1918, some Britishers should be resurrecting the seventeenth-century term *commonwealth* to describe what they wanted the British Empire to become, and that some Americans should be adopting titles from the Solemn League and Covenant to describe the new international organization which they were launching. For the political thought of the seventeenth century is a common inheritance that binds modern Britishers and Americans together.

After 1783 the British Empire and the American republic went their separate ways. In the century that followed, a second British Empire was gradually built up by trade and settlement in Canada and the other British North American colonies, in the Caribbean area, in Australia and New Zealand; and by trade and war in India, South East Asia, and various parts of Africa. In 1837, just after the accession of young Queen

Victoria, the British public was momentarily shocked out of the fit of absence of mind in which this process had been carried on. News came of rebellions round about Montreal and Toronto in the colonies of Lower and Upper Canada. Was a second American Revolution in the making? The idea that colonies, when they reach a certain stage in their growth, will inevitably demand independence and separation lay not very far back in the minds of most nineteenth-century Englishmen after the unfortunate experiences of their ancestors in the years 1765-1783. But the two Canadian rebellions were petty, local affairs. They were easily suppressed, because British American colonial opinion was overwhelmingly loyal. It took Englishmen a long time in the nineteenth century to appreciate the passionate determination of their present British American colonists not to leave the British Empire.

Lord Durham, sent out by the British government to investigate what had been going on in the Canadas, propounded in his famous Report of 1839 the constitutional basis on which a permanent liberal empire could be built up. In this greatest state paper in the history of the Second Empire he proposed the establishment of "Responsible Government" in the colonies.[3] Just as

3. The standard edition of Lord Durham's Report is that edited by Sir Charles Lucas (3 vols.; Oxford, 1912). A useful abridged

Britain was now governed under the monarchy by a Cabinet responsible to a popularly elected House of Commons, so colonial governors should be instructed that it was their duty henceforth in each colony to take the advice of a responsible colonial cabinet, which should hold office as long as it could maintain a majority in the colonial legislative assembly. This procedure, Durham maintained, would restore political peace in the colonies and would preserve the imperial connection by removing colonial grievances. The idea turned out to be creative. Everything that has happened in the political transformation of the British Empire since 1839 stems from this seminal idea of Responsible Government.

Durham had come out to Canada predisposed to take the side of the colonial agitators for reform. He was a radical Whig, who had helped to draft the Reform Bill of 1832 and who had wanted to go further in the direction of democracy than his colleagues had been willing to go. He was a Benthamite, who believed that the duty of the statesman is to seek the greatest happiness of the greatest number and who easily accepted the demand that the majority in a colony should determine how it should be governed. But the particular form that colonial self-government should take

---

text of the Report was published by Sir Reginald Coupland (Oxford, 1945).

was suggested to him after his arrival in Canada by Robert Baldwin, of Toronto, one of the leading Upper Canadian reformers. The beauty of the idea was its simplicity. Let the colonies simply take over the British cabinet form of government. Baldwin exaggerated the degree to which modern cabinet government had developed in Britain by the 1830's; but reformers would usually be ineffective if they did not oversimplify. In the decade after 1839, Responsible Government for the white colonies was accepted as practical politics both in the colonies and in Britain itself.

It is worth while to pause over Durham and his liberal contemporaries in Britain and the colonies. Why was this liberal imperialism successful in the decade 1839-1849, whereas in the decade of 1765-1776 liberal ideas about empire were rejected by British governments and British public opinion? One main difference between the two decades was that the American Revolution took place before the second crisis in the Empire blew up. In a way, the Second British Empire was a by-product of the American Revolution, because Englishmen had been deeply impressed by that experience with the necessity of making concessions to colonial demands if these proved to be firm and persistent. There should be statues to George Washington in all the Dominion capitals, not merely in London.

By the 1830's, also, there was a new atmosphere in Britain itself. The industrial revolution was producing a new Britain. The British people were making over their own domestic political institutions. Reform was in the air. A reformed Parliament was sitting at Westminster, run by political parties which were no longer merely the parliamentary factions of the eighteenth century, but were acquiring a popular base in constituencies with wider electorates. Public opinion outside Parliament was beginning to operate much more directly upon politics, as was shown by the agitation for parliamentary reform itself, the antislavery movement, the Chartist movement, the anti-Corn Law League. An England which was beginning to move towards democracy found sympathetic understanding with frontier colonies much easier than did the England of George III, Lord North, and Dr. Samuel Johnson.

One of the first public acts of that little group of obscure London workingmen who drafted the Charter in the late 1830's was to issue an address welcoming the Canadian rebels of 1837 as brothers. Among their social betters in London, the argument as to the necessity of preserving a final central sovereign authority in full control of the Empire if the Empire were not to disintegrate, the argument that was so effective in eighteenth-century England, was brushed aside in laughter in the

1840's. Charles Buller invented his comic figure, "Mr. Mothercountry," that anonymous, irresponsible bureaucrat in a back room in the Colonial Office who made the real decisions about Imperial policy, whereas neither the British Colonial Secretary, the British Cabinet, the British Parliament, nor the British electorate were well-informed enough or interested enough to undertake the responsibility for the day-to-day government of distant overseas possessions.[4]

It needs also to be emphasized that this political liberalism of the 1830's and 1840's, this willingness to allow colonists to take responsibility for their own affairs, would not have won the day had it not been supported by a great contemporary movement of economic liberalism. By the 1840's Britain had become the workshop of the world. The success of her industrialized economy, the sustenance of her rapidly increasing population, depended on her ability to sell her products in world-wide markets not restricted to narrow national or imperial areas. The Manchester School was educating Englishmen to understand that if they wanted to sell all the manufactured goods they were equipped to produce they must be willing to buy foodstuffs and raw materials from all over

4. Buller's book of 1840, *Responsible Government for Colonies*, which introduced Mr. Mothercountry to the public, is reprinted in Edward Murray Wrong, *Charles Buller and Responsible Government* (Oxford, 1926).

the world.   Britain began to think of the whole
world as an economic unit, all its parts bound together in a great network of interdependence
through trade and investment.   Adam Smith, who
had published his *Wealth of Nations* in the *annus
mirabilis* of 1776 but had not been listened to then,
now at last came into his own.   In 1846 the Anti-
Corn Law League brought about the repeal of
the Corn Laws, to be followed in 1849 by the
repeal of the Navigation Acts, the basis of the old
mercantile Empire.

A country intent on world trade was no longer
so interested in maintaining exclusive control of
the trade of its colonies, and so no longer so interested in tight political control over them.   A
world of freely trading interdependent national
units would also be a peaceful world; and so em-
pires would no longer be needed.   Economic
liberalism and political liberalism went together.
The white Dominions should erect statues to
Richard Cobden and John Bright as well as to
George Washington.

There are several other points to be made about
Durham and the Victorian liberals.   Durham was
one of a very small group of men of great faith
who believed that this liberal policy was the very
thing that would preserve the Empire.   They were
liberals and imperialists at the same time.   Most
Englishmen of the time, however, saw responsible

government and free trade as meaning the ultimate withering away of the Empire. They looked forward to the day when Canadians would go the way of the original American colonists to separate independence. Some of them welcomed this future, and some felt rather sad about it, but all felt it their moral duty, since colonial independence was bound to come, to make friendly concessions to the colonies as demanded, so that when the day of separation did come there would be none of the strife and bitterness that had marked the tragic experience of the 1760's and 1770's. Manchester School liberals welcomed the approach of colonial independence because they assigned an almost mystic value to nationalism as such.[5]

It is pertinent to quote here from Goldwin Smith's book, *The Empire*, published in 1863. Smith was regius professor of history in Oxford at this time and a friend of Cobden and Bright. A few years later he came out to teach history at the newly founded Cornell University, and eventually settled in Toronto in 1871. His book on the Empire contains the pure milk of Manchester liberalism.

England has long promised herself the honour of becoming the mother of free nations. Is it not time that the

5. Carl Adolf Bodelsen, *Studies in Mid-Victorian Imperialism* (New York, 1925); Robert Livingston Schuyler, *The Fall of the Old Colonial System* (New York, 1945); Rita Hinden, *Empire and After* (London, 1949).

promise should be fulfilled? . . . We are keeping the Colonies in a perpetual state of political infancy, and preventing the gristle of their frames from being matured and hardened into bone. . . . We have given them all that we have to give—our national character, our commercial energy, our aptitude for law and government, our language. . . . We have given them the essence of our constitution—free legislation, self-taxation, ministerial responsibility, personal liberty, trial by jury. The accidents of that constitution—the relics of the feudal mould in which it was wrought—we can no more give them than we can give them our history or our skies. . . . England is a European aristocracy, Canada is an American democracy. . . . I am no more against Colonies than I am against the solar system. I am against dependencies, when nations are fit to be independent. . . . But grant that Canada cannot stand as a nation by herself, it is with a nation in America, not with a nation in Europe, that she must ultimately blend. . . . There is but one way to make Canada impregnable, and that is to fence her round with the majesty of an independent nation.[6]

We can see now that the Manchester liberals were wrong in linking colonial independence with separation from the Empire. But they were right in foreseeing that the colonies would insist on going on to full national sovereignty. We should pay them the tribute of recognizing that the peaceful development of the modern Commonwealth would not have been possible but for these Victorian liberal imperial pessimists, who doubted whether the Empire had a future at all.

6. *The Empire*, pp. 1, 3, 97, 104, 123, 134, 2.

Patriotic imperial historians are wont to list as Empire-builders all those later imperial enthusiasts, from Benjamin Disraeli to Joseph Chamberlain and his disciples, who tried to make the Empire into something that it obstinately refused to become, a politically and economically consolidated state.[7] The real empire builders were the Victorian liberals, most of whom did not believe in empire, and their colonial liberal disciples such as Sir Wilfred Laurier in Canada. If there had not been so many heretics in the Empire of yesterday, there would be no Commonwealth today. And the first heretics, we should keep reminding ourselves, were the Americans of the 1770's,

7. Disraeli's Crystal Palace speech of 1872 is usually taken as laying down the program of the new imperialism of the later part of the nineteenth century. After trying to convict his Liberal opponents of an attempt to destroy the Empire, Disraeli went on: "Not that I for one object to self-government; I cannot conceive how our distant Colonies can have their affairs administered except by self-government. But self-government, in my opinion, when it was conceded, ought to have been conceded as part of a great policy of Imperial consolidation. It ought to have been accompanied by an Imperial tariff, by securities for the people of England for the enjoyment of the unappropriated lands which belonged to the Sovereign as their trustee, and by a military code which should have precisely defined the means and the responsibilities by which the Colonies should be defended, and by which, if necessary, this country should call for aid from the colonies themselves. It ought, further, to have been accompanied by the institution of some representative council in the metropolis, which would have brought the Colonies into constant and continuous relations with the Home Government." The specific points in this program are precisely those which have been rejected by later experience in the Commonwealth.

though these were heretics to such an extreme that they excommunicated themselves.

Free trade turned out in the long run to be an empire-building instrument, though when it was adopted it hit the colonies a severe blow by depriving their wheat and timber and sugar of protection in British markets. The spectacular expansion of the British free-trade industrialized economy in the nineteenth century produced an ever-growing metropolitan market for everything that the colonies had to sell. Whereas, in the eighteenth century, the colonies had been compelled against their will by the mercantile system to canalize their trade to British ports, and so became rebellious, in the nineteenth century the new colonies traded naturally and spontaneously with Britain, since it was the best market for their foodstuffs and raw materials and the best source for the manufactured products that they did not yet produce themselves. British capital, accumulated out of the profits of British world trade, poured into the colonies to speed up their economic development. At the same time, an unprecedented stream of emigrants poured out from British ports to people the waste spaces in the colonies. Thus the imperial connection in this liberal century came to seem a natural thing. It profited all parties to it. This long experience of living and working together in a free, friendly, and profitable partnership lies behind the success of the modern Commonwealth.

So far we have considered those parts of the Empire settled by white people. The picture was not nearly so lovely in the other parts; in fact, what the nineteenth century mainly produced there was a sprawling mass of colonial slums. It is also true, however, that the spirit of liberal humanitarianism, becoming more marked as the century went on, had its effect on the dependent Empire as well as in social politics at home. Manchester liberals constituted themselves as a kind of conscience of the Empire.[8] They began to ask inconvenient questions about what British traders and British armies were up to in Africa and Asia. They raised the ultimate question of the moral justification of empire over backward peoples. They drew attention to the seamy side of opium wars in China and little British expeditions up African rivers. They denounced the Boer War as a hypocritical attempt to grab valuable gold and diamond territories in South Africa under the pretense of pressing for the political rights of the Uitlanders in the Transvaal.

At the close of the century and of Queen Victoria's reign a vulgar, blatant Kipling-Chamberlain type of expansionist imperialism seemed to sweep over the nation. The intellectual heirs of

8. John Atkinson Hobson, *Richard Cobden, the International Man* (New York, 1919).

Cobden and Bright helped to discredit this movement and to bring to office the Liberal government
of 1906.[9]   The Liberals gave Responsible Government to the recently conquered Boer communities
of the Transvaal and the Orange Free State; in
the Morley-Minto reforms they started India
on the road to self-government.   A Manchester
liberal, John Atkinson Hobson, in 1902, wrote the
classical liberal attack upon modern imperialism in
his famous book *Imperialism*.   If the Commonwealth today is proving acceptable to Asiatic and
African peoples, one of the main reasons is the
long tradition of nineteenth-century British liberal
anti-imperialism.

The political framework of the nineteenth-century liberal Empire with a predominantly white
population was Responsible Government.   When
Durham made his famous recommendation in 1839
he did not mean by it full national self-government.   He took for granted a large continuing
measure of imperial control over the colonies.   He
took this for granted so thoroughly that he did
not think it necessary to argue the question at
length, devoting only two sentences to it in his
Report.   "The matters which so concern us (i.e.

9. Leonard Trelawney Hobhouse's book, *Democracy and Reaction*, published in 1904 at a moment when British liberalism
seemed to have reached its lowest fortunes, gives a good picture
of how the new combination of mass-democracy and imperialism
struck a twentieth-century Manchester liberal.

the imperial government)", he wrote, "are very few. The constitution of the form of government —the regulation of foreign relations, and of trade with the mother country, the other British Colonies, and foreign nations—and the disposal of the public lands, are the only points on which the mother country requires a control." Responsible Government, that is, in its original conception involved a kind of dyarchy. Certain subjects, purely local domestic concerns, were "transferred" to the control of colonial legislatures; the great imperial interests were "reserved" to the control of the British Parliament.[10]

The success of this experiment, as we can now see, depended on the fact that the line between the transferred local subjects and the reserved imperial subjects was never drawn by statute and was never clearly defined. In the Second Empire no colony challenged the ultimate overriding legal sovereignty of the Parliament at Westminster, and thus no such crisis as that of the 1770's ever developed. But gradually, down to 1931, when the Statute of Westminster finally abolished this sovereignty,

10. Lionel Curtis invented the word *dyarchy*. In his book on Indian government in 1920, which he entitled *Dyarchy*, he devised a scheme for the gradual application of Responsible Government to India. Certain functions of government in the Indian provinces were to be "transferred" to the control of ministers responsible to the provincial legislature; certain others were to be "reserved" for a time to the control of the irresponsible British governor.

which by that time was seldom exercised, Durham's four reserved subjects were transferred bit by bit to the control of colonial legislatures. The point to be understood is that Responsible Government was successful because it turned out to be a flexible, elastic formula, making possible continuous change along with the preservation of continuity. The constitutional secret of the British Empire-Commonwealth is this British genius for avoiding definition. Canadians and other overseas Britishers claim to have inherited this genius to the full. Hence that feeling of serene, effortless intellectual superiority, which you may have observed in our dealings with Americans.

The whole constitutional and political evolution of the Second Empire into the Commonwealth can be summed up by tracing what happened to Durham's four reservations. There is time only to sketch that story here. Public lands were handed over to the Responsible-Government colonies at once in the 1840's and have continued to be mismanaged by them ever since according to their own sweet will. This has made impossible the realization of one of the dreams of Durham and his mentor, Edward Gibbon Wakefield: a great centrally directed scheme of emigration from the overcrowded mother country to the empty lands of the colonies. "The constitution of the form of government" still remains, in the case of Canada, in

the control of the British Parliament, since amend-
ment of the Canadian constitution, the British
North America Act, still has to be sought there.
But the British Parliament has long been accustomed to pass without question such amendments
as are requested by Canada. Australia and South
Africa, coming along later with their constitutions,
made provision for the location of the amending
power within their own boundaries. The final
judicial interpretation of the colonial constitutions
long remained with the Judicial Committee of the
Privy Council in London, but this also has disappeared under slow pressure.

The other two reservations, the control over
colonial trade and the control over defense and
foreign policy, have involved a great deal more
history. After the repeal of the Navigation Acts
in 1849 the self-governing colonies were left free
to make their own tariffs, but it was expected that
they would follow the example of the United
Kingdom in moving towards free trade. When
Canada in the 1850's moved in the opposite direction, there was a considerable amount of controversy. It was nothing less than indecent, said an
indignant protest from the Sheffield Chamber of
Commerce, that a colony should be practising protection while the mother country was practising
free trade. But in 1859 the Canadian government
won its point, that control over fiscal policy was

an essential part of Responsible Government. This was the first main step taken by any colony in expanding the meaning of Responsible Government. After Confederation, Canada definitely settled on a permanent policy of protection, and most of the other Responsible Government colonies went the same way. Gradually also they proceeded not merely to regulate their trade by tariffs, but to enter into direct trade negotiations with foreign countries. While Canada in 1897 gave a special preference in her tariff schedules to British imports, and the other Dominions followed suit, this did not lead, as the Chamberlainites in Britain hoped, to a closely co-ordinated British economic empire. Colonial economic nationalism, with its ambitions towards an industrialized economy, was too strong.

Taking over responsibility for the management of defense and foreign policy was a slower process. The mother country pressed in the 1850's that the burden of local defense in the colonies should be assumed by the colonies themselves as an essential part of the responsibility involved in Responsible Government. By the 1870's most British red-coats had been withdrawn from the self-governing colonies. But the British Navy still undertook the defense of the Empire as a whole, and the British Foreign Office continued to conduct its foreign policy. Before 1914 the colonies had sent contingents to fight in the Boer War; Australia and New Zealand had started naval forces of their own, to be integrated with the British Navy in wartime.   Imperial Conferences were giving colonial governments some opportunity to consult with the imperial authorities about these questions of defense and foreign policy.   But in 1914 the colonies were taken automatically into war by the policy of the British Foreign Secretary, over which they had no real control.   They were, that is, still colonies.   The great advance in this field, which transformed the Empire into the Commonwealth, was not to come till after 1914.

It must be remembered, of course, that behind all these gradual developments in the transfer of reserved powers to colonial governments lay another great change, namely, the emergence of three great colonial nations.   In 1867 four little British American colonies united to form the "new nationality" of Canada, which quickly expanded in a few years into a Dominion stretching from the Atlantic to the Pacific.   In 1900 the six Australian colonies united into the Commonwealth of Australia.   In 1910 the two old British colonies in South Africa, Cape Colony and Natal, united with the recently conquered Boer republics of the Transvaal and Orange Free State to form the Union of South Africa.   Inevitably, these new colonial nations were able to speak with a louder voice to the Colonial Office than had the separate little parochial colonies out of which they had formed themselves. Inevitably, the wine of nineteenth-century nationalism excited them to speak with that louder voice. The surprising thing was not that this nationalism should have shown itself within the Empire, but that it should have been so slow in reaching its full strength. That it did not become separatist or revolutionary is the best proof of the generosity of British nineteenth-century liberalism.

We have seen that Durham's conception of Responsible Government in 1839 was distinctly limited. At the same time, however, he had a vision of a future Canadian nationality. Clearly, he did not mean his four limitations to last indefinitely. In fact, he saw in his mind's eye the future Canadian nation before it had come within the range of vision of most British American colonists themselves. While in Canada, Durham was much impressed by the more advanced state of civilization in the American states to the south. He came also to realize the tremendous attractive force which this American civilization must have upon British Americans. "If we wish to prevent the extension of this influence," he said, "it can only be done by raising up for the North American colonist some nationality of his own; by elevating these small and unimportant communities into a

society having some objects of a national importance; and by thus giving their inhabitants a country which they will be unwilling to see absorbed
even into one more powerful." There you have
the reason why Canadians have always been firm
adherents of the British Empire-Commonwealth.
Their membership in it has enabled them since
1839 to grow from small and unimportant communities into a society having some objects of a
national importance.

Durham's vision, however, had one great limi-
tation. English Canadians revere his memory because he recommended Responsible Government.
Our fellow Canadians of French stock denounce
him because he recommended the Anglifying of
the French Canadians. He declared that the
French had no qualities that made them worthy
of survival as a distinct communal group in British
America. He recommended the Union of English-
speaking Upper Canada with French-speaking
Lower Canada, so that an English majority by
steady pressure might submerge the French in an
Anglo-Saxon civilization. The British Empire to
him was to be an English empire.

Of course Responsible Government did not work
out this way. The French organized themselves
as a solid minority group to protect their interests,
and they have been brilliantly successful. Ever
since the late 1840's, when Responsible Govern-

ment was put into practice in Canada, members of
the French-Canadian group have sat to the right
of Mr. Speaker in the Canadian legislature and
Parliament, save for ten unhappy years from 1911
to 1921. That is, they have formed part of the
government. They have brought it about that no
major decision in Canadian policy can be taken
without their consent. They have established, in
other words, the principle of concurrent majorities.
Every French Canadian is a practising John C.
Calhoun.

The political success of the French Canadians in
winning full participation in the government of
Canada was the first decisive step towards what has
become the modern multi-racial Commonwealth.
In 1837, the year that Queen Victoria came to the
throne, there was a rebellion in French Canada.
In 1897, sixty years later, when she celebrated her
diamond jubilee, the Prime Minister attending the
celebration from her senior self-governing Dominion, Canada, was Wilfrid Laurier, a French
Canadian. He was the forerunner of a Botha in
South Africa, a Nehru in India, and a Nkruma in
the Gold Coast.

One might go on with different illustrations of
the liberal basis of the nineteenth-century Empire.
Let us conclude with an illustration of the Victorian liberal spirit taken from the correspondence
between two eminent Victorians in 1874. In that

year the Governor-General of Canada in Ottawa was Lord Dufferin, a Liberal appointee of the Gladstone government. The Colonial Secretary in London was Lord Carnarvon, a Conservative member of the Disraeli government. In spite of party differences, the two men were close personal friends. Their correspondence from 1874 to 1878, which I have just had the pleasure of editing,[11] gives a fascinating picture of that Victorian spirit of tolerance, accommodation, and good will which forms the background of the modern Commonwealth. Dufferin and Carnarvon were both strong imperialists with a somewhat exalted idea of the function of the mother country in guiding young, immature colonists, and they had a certain amount of trouble with the Canadian nationalist Liberal government of Alexander Mackenzie. But they were also, like most Victorian Englishmen, liberals with a small *l*. The letter of Dufferin from which I quote contains an able exposition of this liberalism.

You may depend upon my doing my very best both to weld this Dominion into an Imperium solid enough to defy all attraction from its powerful neighbour across the line, and to perpetuate its innate loyalty to the Mother Country. . . .

But though union with the Republic has become an obsolete idea, I cannot help suspecting that there is a

11. Cornelius William deKiewiet and Frank H. Underhill, eds., *Dufferin-Carnarvon Correspondence 1874-1878* (Toronto, 1955).

growing desire amongst the younger generation to regard "Independence" as their ultimate destiny. Nor do I think that this novel mode of thought will be devoid of benefit, provided it remains for the next twenty or thirty years a vague aspiration, and is not prematurely converted into a practical project. Hitherto there has been a lack of self-assertion and self-confidence amongst Canadians in forcible contrast with the sentiments which animate our friends to the south of us:—now however, the consolidation of the Provinces . . . has stimulated their imagination. . . .

If then this growing consciousness of power should stimulate their pride in the resources and future of their country, nay even if it should sometimes render them jealous of any interference on the part of England with their Parliamentary autonomy, I do not think we shall have any cause of complaint. On the contrary, we should view with favour the rise of a high-spirited, proud, national feeling amongst them. Such a sentiment would neither be antagonistic to our interests, nor inimical to the maintenance of the tie which now subsists between us. The one danger to be avoided is that of converting this healthy and irrepressible growth of a localized patriotism, into a condition of morbid suspicion or irritability, by any exhibition of jealousy, or by the capricious exercise of authority on the part of the Imperial Government. Nothing has more stimulated the passionate affection with which Canada now clings to England, than the consciousness that the maintenance of the connection depends on her own free-will. . . .

Our chief object should be to keep things pretty much as they are for the next twenty years, and although in time of course some change is inevitable, it may then be expected to be of a nature, and to take place under conditions which will reward us for our wise and temperate government.[12]

12. *Ibid.*, pp. 34-36. These reflections of Dufferin about the

As we shall see, the transformation of the Empire into the Commonwealth in the twentieth century was of a nature and took place under conditions which rewarded British statesmen for their wise and temperate government in the nineteenth century.

---

future were occasioned by the founding in Toronto of the "Canada First" movement, with aspirations towards Canadian independence, under the inspiration of Goldwin Smith, who had settled in Toronto in 1871.

2

The First Commonwealth

THE SUBJECT of this lecture is the First Commonwealth, the new form of association among the British self-governing nations which emerged from their experience in fighting World War I together. But, as is the way with historians, there is a long historical introduction before I reach the year 1917.

The first lecture was not intended to interpret the history of the British Empire-Commonwealth as an example of an inspired British dialectic: thesis, the old Empire of the eighteenth century; antithesis, the Canadian rebellions of 1837; synthesis, Responsible Government leading to Commonwealth. There have been rather too many books written by Britons—Britons overseas as well as Britons in Oxford and London—who, in their ecstasy over this supreme exhibition of British abstract reason, tend to prostrate themselves before this dialectic in an attitude of truly German philosophic adoration. Actually, historically, what took place in the Empire was a process of trial and error, in which some pragmatic, experimental, open-minded, liberal statesmen felt their way towards a conclusion which none of them saw very clearly and which in fact became clear only in our own generation. We must beware of the temptation to talk as if the conclusion has been reached even in our day. Adam Smith warned his contemporaries that too many of them were deluding themselves that they had an empire, whereas all they really had was the project of an empire. What we are dealing with today is still the project of a commonwealth.

It is usually said, quite correctly, that the War of 1914-1918 was the point in history at which the self-governing white colonies of European stock broke their way out from their colonial chrysalis, tested their wings, and began to fly freely as full-fledged sovereign nation-states. By the time the peace treaties were signed in 1919, they had achieved a new status in the Empire and a new status in the world at large. But the real watershed, the point at which the Responsible-Government colonies began to become conscious of wider responsibilities than those of purely local, domestic, municipal self-government was the South African War of 1899. It was then they entered on the stage of world-power politics. They sent contingents to fight in a war that was part of the imperialist struggle of European powers for the division of Africa, a war in which the overseas colonies themselves were not directly concerned. By their action they recognized in effect, even if colonial public opinion was not quite clear about it at the moment, that they as well as the mother country had some responsibility for the maintenance of British power in the world and for the purposes to which that power was directed.

There was to be no drawing back from the precedent thus set. When Sir Wilfrid Laurier, the Canadian Prime Minister, sent the first Canadian contingent in the fall of 1899, without consulting the Canadian Parliament or the Canadian people, he had an Order-in-Council passed stating that this action should not constitute a precedent. The precedent, indignantly replied Henri Bourassa in Parliament, is the accomplished fact. And Bourassa, presenting himself as "a thorough British liberal," gave voice to the long and persistent French-Canadian protest against entanglement in British imperialist wars. "If," he said, "we send 2,000 men, and spend $2,000,000 to fight two nations aggregating a population of 250,000 souls, how many men shall we send and how many millions shall we expend to fight a first-class power or a coalition of powers? And it is no doubt to first-class powers and to possible coalitions that the

lesson and the warning were meant to be given. . . .
It is the starting point of a new policy which opens
a serious point of view on the future of this country. The point of view may be glorious for those
who aspire after military honours. It may inspire
to rhetoricians fine sounding periods, or lyric stan-
zas to lyric rhymers. But it prepares a gloomy
future for the farming and labouring classes of this
country."

Bourassa was the first Canadian public man to
force his fellow-citizens to face up to the implica-
tions of their position in an Empire over whose
international policies they had no control. Down
to 1899 the colonies on the whole had lived their
lives shielded by the British Navy from the direct
impact of world power politics. They had been
accustomed to accept the Pax Britannica of the
nineteenth century as a part of the order of nature.
The South African War started their education
in the facts of life in a hard world, where peace
could no longer be counted on.

Since then the controversy begun by Bourassa
in Canada as to the relation of his community to
the Empire and to the world has gone on continu-
ously in one form or another in all the Dominions.
Some of their citizens have taken refuge at times
in isolationism or neutralism. Their isolationism
depended on the assumption that British power
would continue to be effective in making impossible

any aggression from outside upon themselves. But these were a minority.

Another minority, at the opposite extreme of opinion, were stimulated by danger to demand a close organic unity with Great Britain. Colonial nationalism was too strong for this minority. In the end the majority in the middle worked out with a similar majority in Britain the strangely unorganized form of association which is called the Commonwealth. The Commonwealth has none of the precise commitments of a formal alliance, yet it functions as an unwritten treaty of mutual guaranty. The paradox about this Commonwealth relationship is that in times of peace and security there does not seem to be anything much in common between the members of the Commonwealth except some rather repetitious rhetoric about their unity of spirit; but in times of danger they work together like a well-drilled team. Americans find this spectacle hard to comprehend, because they cannot understand a team without a coach. The members of the Commonwealth team, and especially the Canadian member, have always refused to train or to play under a coach.

Before 1914 several developments besides the South African War had taken place, which are worth attention because they form significant features of the background out of which the new Commonwealth emerged in the years 1917-1919.

In Britain itself, from the 1870's on, there had developed a strong reaction against the Manchester, Little England ideas about the Empire that had been dominant in the middle of the century.[1] The colonies began to take on a romantic color. Englishmen began to dream dreams about them. The idea of abandoning them became more and more distasteful. From the depression of 1873 on, Britain was finding herself faced by ever-increasing competition in world markets, as the rest of the Western World went through the industrial revolution, especially the two new giants, Germany and the United States. Imperial markets which she might be able to reserve for herself against foreign intrusion began to look much more attractive. At the same time, Bismarckian Germany was upsetting the European balance of power, and when William II began to press German ambitions beyond the European continent, Britain was driven to worry more and more about her strategic security. In defense as well as in trade the Empire might come to her help.

This new imperialist trend resulted, in 1887, in the first Colonial Conference. On the occasion of Queen Victoria's golden jubilee, representatives of the colonial governments were invited to meet with the imperial authorities to talk over common

1. John Ecclesfield Tyler, *The Struggle for Imperial Unity 1868-1895* (London, 1938).

problems. The invitation started a new institution. The name Colonial Conference was changed in 1907 to Imperial Conference, the word *colony* having by this time become unpopular in colonies like Canada, which were beginning to talk and think of themselves as nations. These Imperial Conferences continued at irregular intervals till 1937, just before World War II. By that time they were apparently becoming a little too regular and formal for Canadian and South African tastes. At any rate, since the war their place has been taken by very informal meetings called Prime Ministers' Conferences, in which the delegates meet privately without any agenda or any adequate report of their proceedings.

After one of these contemporary conferences, our Canadian Secretary of State for External Affairs, Mr. Lester Pearson, remarked, in discussing the very colorless and incomprehensible report that issued from it, that if there had been press releases in 1215 at the time of Magna Carta, the official report of that famous Runnymede meeting would have run: "A full and friendly discussion took place on the subject of feudal rights, and the barons made some recommendations to His Majesty."

All attempts since 1887 to transform these conferences into some regular constitutional organ of government have been defeated, chiefly by a firm

Canadian veto. They remain conferences, which cannot pass resolutions committing anybody to anything against his will, but which, as we can now well see, have a growing value in the opportunity they give to Commonwealth statesmen to exchange ideas and to get to know each other.

Americans might be interested to compare the history of these conferences with that of the conferences among the twenty-one American republics which started at almost the same time, in 1889. Canada has steadfastly refused to join this pan-American enterprise, which is certainly much more elaborate, which has a secretariat, and which indulges in much more high-flying Latin rhetoric and much more American constitution-making than suits the taste of Britishers, but which seems to us much less real in its practical achievements.

In 1879 Canada took the initiative in another step which has had important consequences. The government of Sir John Macdonald proposed that, since the new Dominion of Canada, stretching from the Atlantic to the Pacific, had so much business to discuss and transact with Britain, a Canadian official should be appointed to handle the business in London and that he should function as a quasi-diplomatic representative of Canada at the Court of St. James. The Canadian government was politely snubbed over this proposal and told that a colony like Canada could not equate itself with a sovereign foreign power in the capital of the Empire. But it was agreed that an official should be appointed, to be called the Canadian High Comsioner.[2] Britain did not reciprocate with a British High Commissioner in Ottawa, since she had the Governor-General there. Down to 1914 the Canadian High Commissioner did not amount to much in London. He did not achieve that diplomatic status which the Canadian government had suggested until the 1930's, when Mr. Vincent Massey was appointed by the King government.

But the somewhat inconspicuous start of the High Commissionership is important. Today the member states of the Commonwealth are all represented by High Commissioners in each other's capitals, who are ambassadors in all but name. In London the High Commissioners not only look after the individual business, each of his own country; they also meet regularly and frequently in conference with the British Secretary of State for Commonwealth Affairs. It is difficult to overestimate the importance of the influence exercised by this habit of consultation among the Prime Ministers, High Commissioners, and other officials of the Commonwealth governments.

The revived imperial enthusiasm in Britain,

2. On the evolution of the High Commissionership, the Department of External Affairs, and the diplomatic service, see Harold Gordon Skilling, *Canadian Representation Abroad* (Toronto, 1945).

which liberals were apt to denounce as jingoism, reached its height just at the end of the nineteenth century, on the eve of the Boer War. Its popular spokesman was Rudyard Kipling, "that brassy Briton" as some unkind American once called him, with his talk of taking up the white man's burden and of lesser breeds without the law. The man who tried to institutionalize the new spirit in a new, closely consolidated empire was Joseph Chamberlain, who became Colonial Secretary in 1895. Chamberlain and Kipling, it may be noted, both appeared in Britain at the opening of the modern period of mass-democracy—a fact which is worth some reflection.

At the two Colonial Conferences over which he presided, in 1897 and 1902, Chamberlain drove hard to persuade the colonial Prime Ministers to agree to his conception of a more closely united Empire. In 1902, trying to take advantage of the imperial enthusiasm kindled by the South African War, he told them, applying Matthew Arnold's poetry to the British Empire, that the weary (British) titan struggled under the too vast orb of his fate, and he invited the vigorous young Dominions to help bear the burden. But all his suggestions of some new central imperial council, of a colonial contribution to the Royal Navy, of colonial militia units trained and earmarked for service in the next war, were rejected by the Canadian Prime Minister, Laurier. In effect, Chamberlain was defeated by Laurier, since the two South Pacific Dominions were much more sympathetic to his proposals.

After this, Chamberlain took up the cause of Imperial Preference, proposing to bind the Empire countries more closely together by economic bonds and hoping that economic integration would lay the foundation for later political and military co-operation. This proposal, however, involved Britain's abandonment of free trade, a step which the British electorate in the 1906 election decisively refused to take. Laurier assisted also in this defeat of Chamberlain, for, although in 1897 he had given a preference to British goods in Canadian markets, he now refused to commit himself to further increased British preferences if Chamberlain should secure a preference for Canadian wheat in British markets. Canadian economic nationalism, which was protectionist, and British economic nationalism, which was free trade—both equally self-centered—frustrated this effort of Chamberlain to go back to the old mercantile Empire of before 1846.

There was to be a prolonged aftermath to this Chamberlain-Laurier struggle. Thirty years later, at the Ottawa Conference of 1932, it looked as if a second Chamberlain, Neville, who had as Chancellor of the Exchequer brought back protection in England, would at last see his father's dream realized. At Ottawa the nations of the Commonwealth worked out a complex network of bilateral trade agreements avowedly aimed at shutting foreigners, especially Americans, out of Empire markets. But the glamour soon faded from the Ottawa system. Canada was not willing to give effective preferences to the goods that Britain wanted to export in quantity, i.e., to textiles and to iron and steel products. She did put such items as Scotch bagpipes on the free list, but you cannot build up a working imperial economy on this sour basis.

When the Liberals came back to office in Canada in 1935, King proceeded to substitute for the bilateral British-Canadian agreement of 1932 an intricate triangular trade arrangement between Britain, Canada, and the United States. In fact, the essence of King's general statesmanship, in which he was much more far-seeing than most of his contemporaries, may be said to have been to substitute for the old dual British-Canadian loyalty the new triangular North-Atlantic relationship, which now dominates Canadian external policy.

This defeat of Chamberlainism by Laurier and King was a necessary prelude to the kind of Commonwealth with which we are experimenting today. When Lord Beaverbrook, the last surviving Chamberlainite, dies, we may expect that all that is left of Chamberlainism will be quietly deposited with the Beaverbrook papers to gather dust in the Archives of the University of New Brunswick.[3] This will be true for Canada, at any rate, if not for other parts of the Commonwealth.

The achievement of the Commonwealth in 1917-1919 involved the defeat of another attempt to bind the Empire more closely together, an attempt which, like the Chamberlain campaign, originated in Britain and appealed most strongly to British Conservatives. This was the Round Table movement, inspired by Lionel Curtis and his friends of Lord Milner's kindergarten in South Africa. Curtis became the prophet of a very able group of men, who preached Imperial Federation as the only way to save the Empire amidst the storms of the twentieth century. He pointed out that Dominions like Canada—this was just before 1914—in spite of all their fine talk about being fully self-governing, were still really colonial, because they had no control over the ultimate issues of policy that would determine their future, the

3. The best recent exposition of Chamberlainite aspirations and policies is to be found in Leopold Stennett Amery, *My Political Life* (3 vols.; London, 1953-1955). Mr. Amery was so full of his gospel that he remained blissfully unaware of what was really going on in the minds of citizens of the overseas parts of the Commonwealth. In fact, when he visited them he talked so incessantly that he gave himself no opportunity to listen to their opinions. He was the typical doctrinaire, the perfect doctrinaire, the ideal doctrinaire, the doctrinaire as he exists in the mind of God.

issues of war and peace. These were decided for them by the government of the United Kingdom.

The Curtis argument here was unanswerable. He went on to claim that the Canadian people could acquire control over this vital area of foreign policy only by one of two ways: either by becoming independent, leaving the Empire and setting up as a separate sovereign nation, or by gaining a real share in the making of British policy. Since, obviously, the Canadian people would reject the first alternative, their only choice, if they were not content to remain permanently in the colonial stage, was to achieve full citizenship in the British Commonwealth.

Curtis popularized the use of this new term *commonwealth*. He argued that a Canadian citizen would not be fully self-governing until he had the same responsibility in respect of external affairs, of peace and war, as had a British citizen who lived in England. Hunting about for a new name for the reconstituted Empire, in which Canadians would be equal to Englishmen, he thought of the phrase "A Commonwealth of Nations." But the Curtis Commonwealth, as he developed his argument, was to be a closely knit, single federal state on the model of the United States of America. One of the Round Table heroes was Alexander Hamilton, and Curtis was fond of quoting Washington's sentence, "Influence is not government."

There was to be created, as in 1787, a new entity, a federation of Britain and her Dominions, with a federal parliament in which would sit elected representatives of Britain, Canada, Australia, New Zealand, and South Africa. This parliament would have jurisdiction over defense, foreign policy, and the government of dependencies. Administering the government would be a cabinet on the British model, responsible to the federal parliament.[4]

Curtis and other imperialists presented the idea of Canada's becoming a junior partner in the imperial firm in a most attractive way in the days round about 1914. What was most appealing about it to thoughtful Canadians was that it promised to raise the Canadian vision above petty, parochial local politics, to produce a higher type of Canadian statesmanship. Stephen Leacock was one of these Canadian imperialists, and is worth quoting on this topic. In a brilliant and witty article in the *University Magazine*, April, 1907, then published jointly by three Canadian Universities —McGill, Toronto, and Dalhousie—he wrote:

Now, in this month of April, when the ice is leaving our rivers, the ministers of Canada take ship for this the fourth Colonial Conference at London. What do they go to do? Nay rather, what shall we bid them do? We—the six million people of Canada, unvoiced, untaxed,

4. The Curtis scheme was expounded in *The Problem of the Commonwealth* (London, 1916) and in many articles in the quarterly journal, the *Round Table*, founded by his group.

in the Empire, unheeded in the councils of the world—
we the six million colonials sprawling our over-suckled
infancy across a continent—what shall be our message
to the mother land?   Shall we still whine of our poverty,
still draw imaginary pictures of our thin herds shivering
in the cold blasts of the North, their shepherds huddled
for shelter in the log cabins of Montreal and Toronto?
Shall we still beg the good people of England to bear yet
a little longer, for the poor peasants of their colony, the
burden and heat of the day?   Shall our ministers rehearse
this worn out fiction of our 'acres of snow,' and so sail
home again, still untaxed, to the smug approval of the
oblique politicians of Ottawa?   Or shall we say to the
people of England, 'The time has come; we know and
realize our country.   We will be your colony no longer.
Make us one with you in an Empire, Permanent and
Indivisible.'

This last alternative means what is commonly called
Imperialism.   It means a united system of defence, an
imperial navy for whose support somehow or other the
whole Empire shall properly contribute, and with it an
imperial authority in whose power we all may share. . . .
I, that write these lines, am an Imperialist because I will
not be a Colonial.   This Colonial status is a worn-out, by-
gone thing.   It limits the ideas and circumscribes the patriotism of our people.   It impairs the mental vigor and
narrows the outlook of those that are reared and educated in our midst. . . .

Not Independence then, not annexation, not stagnation; nor yet that doctrine of a little Canada that some
conceive—half in, half out of the Empire, with a mimic
navy of its own; a pretty navy this,—poor two-penny
collection, frolicking on its little way strictly within the
Gulf of St. Lawrence, a sort of silly adjunct to the navy
of the Empire, semi-detached, the better to be smashed
at will.   As well a navy of the Province, or the Parish

home-made for use at home, docked every Saturday in Lake Nipigon!

. . . . Measure not the price. It is not a commercial benefit we buy. We are buying back our honour as Imperial Citizens. . . . Thus stands the case. Thus stands the future of Canada. Find for us something other than mere colonial stagnation, something sounder than independence, nobler than annexation, greater in purpose than a Little Canada. Find us a way. Build us a plan that shall make us, in hope at least, an Empire Permanent and Indivisible.

Alas for the appeals of the Leacocks and the Curtises! The Canadian colonials found another way to achieve that Greater Canada which should include full responsibility for external policy. The Curtis plan was decisively rejected by practically all the responsible leaders throughout the Empire. At the 1911 Imperial Conference the Prime Minister of New Zealand was persuaded to move a resolution in favor of federation, only to be overwhelmed by the opposition of Laurier from Canada, Botha from South Africa, and Asquith from the United Kingdom. True, the outbreak of war in 1914 seemed to Curtis to prove his point finally. Canadians woke up on August 4 to find themselves at war as a result of the policy of the British Foreign Secretary, who was responsible to the British electorate but to no one in Canada. Curtis was right in feeling that Canadians would soon find such a situation intolerable. But they refused to adopt his way out of the difficulty. His fine imaginative title of a Commonwealth of Nations was stolen from him in 1917 by Sir Robert Borden, of Canada, and General Smuts, of South Africa, who proceeded to apply it to another kind of commonwealth altogether.

Federation is an idea which appeals to Americans, who apparently find it difficult to see why their successful federal experience should not be repeated on a broader international scale, or at least repeated by Europeans. Dominion nationalism defeated the idea in the British Empire. Canada and her sister Dominions cherished the autonomy which they had won in the period since Lord Durham's Report, and they were not willing to give up one jot of it to any new supranational imperial authority. Canadians were not willing to place themselves in a position in which, on some important issue of foreign policy, the Canadian delegates might be outvoted by a majority in a federal parliament and committed to action of which they disapproved. On this point all the Dominions have been clear-headed and immovable from the start. The only tolerable form of Commonwealth association to them is one in which each member decides as to the extent of his own obligations and responsibilities and as to the method by which he shall carry them out. Before he decides, he participates in long discussions and consultations with his fellow members. But he decides for himself.

Logicians can easily demonstrate that this loose kind of an association, with every member possessing a Sam Goldwyn freedom to include himself out at any moment, will not work. The answer to them is that the life of the British Commonwealth is not logic but experience. And experience since 1917 has shown that it does work.

Let us pause before going on to consider the Borden-Smuts Commonwealth in more detail. All the ideas about imperial architecture that originated in Great Britain were rejected. The Commonwealth that emerged from the crisis of the First World War was based upon other ideas, propounded by Smuts from South Africa and Borden from Canada, and carried further in the following decades by King from Canada, Hertzog from South Africa, de Valera from Ireland, and Nehru from India. Should one generalize from this—seeing that the original idea of Responsible Government originated nearly a century earlier in Toronto—and conclude that the imaginative, creative ideas come from the periphery of the Empire and that the statesmanship at the center in London shows its highest wisdom when it accepts and works out the suggestions that originate elsewhere? Canadian modesty forbids me to press this point too insistently. At any rate, we now come to the

scheme which was actually adopted, the Commonwealth first officially proposed in 1917 by Borden
and Smuts.

The Prime Minister of Canada in 1914 was the
Conservative Sir Robert Borden. He had proposed in the Canadian Parliament two years earlier
an emergency Canadian contribution of three
dreadnoughts to the British Navy, but he had not
been able to get this through the Canadian Senate.
He had accompanied this naval proposal with a
declaration that if Canada contributed to imperial
defense she must be given a voice in the making
of imperial policy. Down to 1916 the British
government showed a polite but complete deafness
to his thesis. Even when Canadian divisions were
fighting in France, he could get no response from
the Asquith government. But, at the end of 1916,
David Lloyd George became British Prime Min
ister. He immediately formed an inner War Cabinet of five men to devote themselves without
departmental or other distractions to the prosecution of the war. In this War Cabinet he invited
the Dominion Prime Ministers to sit, and early in
1917 the War Cabinet expanded into the Imperial
War Cabinet.

This was an astonishing advance. The Dominions were at one bound raised from colonies to
full partners. Overnight Sir Robert Borden found
his demand for a share in the making of policy

answered in the most complete way, or so it seemed. The result was a certain amount of intellectual intoxication during the exciting months of 1917 and 1918. All the pundits hailed the Imperial War Cabinet as a great epoch-making constitutional innovation, a typical product of pragmatic British statesmanship, the sort of thing that political philosophers in their studies could never have thought of, but which we practical Britishers, when we are up against a critical practical problem, always manage to devise.

Actually, as we can now see, it was not a cabinet at all in any intelligible British sense. A cabinet is a group of ministers under a prime minister who has personally selected them, under whom they come into office as a unit and go out of office as a unit; they are jointly responsible to one legislature, and if an individual minister does not agree with his fellows or with the prime minister he has to resign. The Imperial War Cabinet was not such a body. Lloyd George was responsible to the British Parliament; Sir Robert Borden, to the Canadian, and General Smuts, to the South African Parliament. If Borden should disagree with his colleagues, he did not resign, but continued to press the Canadian point of view; and there was no way of compelling him to accept his colleagues' decisions if he wanted to be obstinate. The Imperial War Cabinet was just the Imperial Con-

ference with a new name, meeting more continu-
ously and dealing with more urgent day-to-day
problems.

But it worked. Its members did not quarrel
or disagree on any major point. At the end of the
war they transferred themselves under a new title,
the British Empire Delegation, to Paris; there
they conducted with the spokesmen of the allied
and associated powers the negotiations that led to
the peace treaties. Borden and Smuts insisted that
the Dominions must play a full part in these
negotiations, must be given original seats on the
new international organization, the League of
Nations, and must through their accredited representatives separately sign the peace treaties. To
these demands they secured first the assent of
Lloyd George and then, sometimes with more difficulty, of President Wilson. Lloyd George agreed
also that before His Britannic Majesty ratified the
treaties each treaty should be submitted to the
Dominion Parliaments as well as to the British
Parliament; only on their approval should it be
ratified.

Thus in these two eventful years between 1917
and 1919 the Dominions achieved a new status
both within the Empire and in the outside world
of international diplomacy. Dominion status was
not quite independent sovereignty, and outsiders
had some difficulty in understanding this new enti-

ty, the British Commonwealth of Nations, which
sometimes presented itself to the world as a single
unit speaking with one voice, that of the British
Empire Delegation, and sometimes dissolved into
half a dozen individual states, as at League meetings in Geneva, each speaking with its own individual national voice.   The essential nature of the
British Commonwealth was a question on which
British experts in constitutional law could split
hairs *ad infinitum*.   In 1921 the *Round Table*
remarked: "How the orthodox believer of today
is to worship the diversity in unity and the unity
in diversity of the British Commonwealth, neither
confounding the persons by undue centralisation,
nor dividing the substance to the point of complete
independence of its parts, is a question which awaits
solution by some Athanasius of Empire who has
not yet appeared and would probably find himself
contra mundum if he did."[5]

In 1917, again on the initiative of Borden and
Smuts, the prime ministers of the Empire, gathered
in conference, passed a resolution attempting to set
forth their conception of what they were doing.

The Imperial War Conference are of opinion that the
readjustment of the constitutional relations of the com-
ponent parts of the Empire is too important and intricate
a subject to be dealt with during the war, and that it
should form the subject of a special Imperial Conference

5. XI, 542.

to be summoned as soon as possible after the cessation of hostilities.

It deems it its duty, however, to place on record its view that any such readjustment, while thoroughly preserving all existing powers of self-government and complete control of domestic affairs, should be based upon a full recognition of the Dominions as autonomous nations of an Imperial Commonwealth, and of India as an important portion of the same, should recognize the right of the Dominions and India to an adequate voice in foreign policy and in foreign relations, and should provide effective arrangements for continuous consultation in all important matters of common Imperial concern, and for such necessary concerted action, founded on consultation, as the several Governments may determine.

Note certain significant words in this Resolution IX: (1) the word *commonwealth* is now first used officially as denoting this new kind of empire, which consists not of a metropolitan power with dependent colonies, but of a group of equal nation-states; (2) India is given a special status, though not yet in any sense self-governing; (3) the Dominions as "autonomous nations" have a right to "an adequate voice in foreign policy"; and (4) Empire foreign policy is henceforth not to be made by the British Foreign Office acting as a sort of trustee for immature colonies; it is to be based on "continuous consultation"; it is to consist of "concerted action founded on consultation."

The equality of which the Dominions now boasted was not quite real. The Dominions had

no trained diplomatic staffs of their own.   Sir
Robert Borden at Paris had hardly any Canadian
experts on whom to rely; he had to depend chiefly
on the trained and skilful officials of the British
Foreign Office.   Beyond this, the equal participation of the Dominions in the making of policy
depended on the continuance of the so-called Imperial War Cabinet.   But, after 1919, the War
Cabinet broke up, and there was no Imperial Peace
Cabinet to take its place.   The last time the British
nations worked as a unit in this form was at the
Washington Naval Disarmament Conference of
1921-1922, when a British Empire Delegation,
exactly like that of 1918-1919 at Paris, attended
under the chairmanship of Arthur James Balfour,
of the United Kingdom.

After this, what we may call the Borden-Smuts
Commonwealth tended to go to pieces.   How
genuinely united it had been during the stress of
war and of peace-making is best shown in the memoirs which the statesmen of those days later published as justifications of themselves.   Each one,
British or American or French, demonstrated about
the statesmen of other countries with whom he had
had to deal that they were either stupid fools or
impossible idealists or slippery opportunists.   Only
the statesmen of the British Commonwealth made
no ugly or unpleasant revelations about each other.

The Borden-Smuts Commonwealth was based upon the assumption that the Commonwealth would continue on the whole to have one united foreign policy, to be worked out henceforth by continuous consultation among its members. But, with peace once established, the urge for continuous consultation lessened and disappeared. The constitutional conference which was provided for in the 1917 resolution was not held. No machinery of consultation took the place of the late Imperial War Cabinet except Imperial Conferences in 1921, 1923, and 1926. In the circumstances, each member-state tended to concentrate upon its own policy in its own region of the world. So the Borden-Smuts Commonwealth slowly disintegrated into the highly decentralized form of association that may be called the King-Hertzog Commonwealth. In the world of the 1920's, when the League of Nations existed to guarantee secure international peace, there did not seem to be much need to worry about a single united Commonwealth policy. Canada under Prime Minister William Lyon Mackenzie King made it clear in a series of incidents that the British Foreign Office could not commit her to anything in Europe and that she was determined to go ahead with her own Canadian policy in relations with the United States in North America. What did these differences matter as long as the League of Nations was there? As somebody remarked in those days, the League of Nations was the *deus ex machina* of the British Commonwealth.

The idea of the King-Hertzog Commonwealth was expounded in the famous Balfour Report of the 1926 Imperial Conference.[6] Speaking of Britain and the self-governing Dominions, it declared: "Their position and mutual relation may be readily defined. They are autonomous Communities within the British Empire, equal in status, in no way subordinate one to another in any aspect of their domestic or external affairs, though united by a common allegiance to the Crown, and freely associated as members of the British Commonwealth of Nations."

This famous definition, it will be seen, stresses the independence of each member state but hardly explains in what their unity consists beyond the fact of their common allegiance to the Crown. The Report admitted that a foreigner might be tempted to think that the formula was devised to make mutual interference impossible rather than to make mutual co-operation easy. But it went on to a declaration of faith that "though every Dominion is now, and must always remain, the sole judge of the nature and extent of its co-

6. The text is in Arthur Berriedale Keith, *Speeches and Documents on the British Dominions, 1918-1931* (London, 1932), I, 161; James Barry Munnik Hertzog was the current Prime Minister of the Union of South Africa.

operation, no common cause will, in our opinion, be thereby imperilled." The puzzled foreigner must have been still further puzzled by the next paragraph, which declared that "while equality of status is thus the root principle of our Inter-Imperial Relations, the principles of equality appropriate to status do not universally extend to function."

What did this piece of Scottish, Balfourian metaphysics mean? A sarcastic Canadian commentator declared that it meant that the Dominions were equal to Britain when standing still, i.e., in status, but not equal when doing anything, i.e., in function. But King and Hertzog were able to bring back the 1926 Report and flourish it as the final victory of Dominion national autonomy, while conservatives in the more 'loyal' parts of the Commonwealth, such as Australia and New Zealand, and in Britain itself, were able to assure each other that the Report said nothing but what all sensible people had always understood anyway.

There were a number of obvious points in which a Dominion was not equal to the United Kingdom. Its government was presided over by a Governor-General sent from Britain; decisions of its courts were subject to appeal to the Judicial Committee of the Imperial Privy Council; its Parliament had not the power to pass extraterritorial legislation, and laws passed by its Parliament were sub-

ject to disallowance by the British authorities. The
Colonial Laws Validity Act of 1865 declared that
any colonial law conflicting with a British law on
the same subject was null and void, and the senior
Dominion, Canada, could get amendments to its
constitution only by having recourse to the British
Parliament, which had originally passed the British
North America Act in 1867. Some of these difficulties had already been cleared away for all practical purposes (e.g., that of the disallowance
power) by the British process of substituting new
constitutional custom for old formal law. The
formal independence of Dominion Parliaments was
established by the Statute of Westminster in 1931.
It was no part of the policy of His Majesty's government in Great Britain, said the Report of 1926,
to maintain controls that were obnoxious to any
Dominion.[7]

These technical internal matters, while fascinating to constitutional experts, need not worry us
here. What determined the future of the Commonwealth was foreign policy, the response of the
British communities to a world plunging once more
towards the catastrophe of war.

After 1931, the assumption on which the King-

7. The nice constitutional issues that arose from the new
"Dominion Status" cannot be properly dealt with without a much
longer discussion than is possible here. For a full and authoritative discussion, see Kenneth Clinton Wheare, *The Statute of
Westminster and Dominion Status* (5th ed.; London, 1952).

Hertzog Commonwealth was based, the assumption of a world enjoying a secure peace, ceased to be true. To quote the once-famous remark of an American commentator after the arrival of Hitler in office, "as 1933 passed into 1934, the world passed from the post-war into the pre-war era." Japanese aggression in Manchuria, Italian aggression in Ethiopia, German aggression in Austria, and the threat of continued German aggression to the point at which Hitler's Third Reich became a danger not only to Britain in Europe but to the overseas Commonwealth countries also—these unexpected challenges were presented to the British countries just when the new Commonwealth system was getting well started. It cannot be pretended that the response down to 1939 was heroic. The remarkable thing was that, while each member was free to make up its own mind and there was no possibility of a central direction of policy, the leadership of Britain under Baldwin and Chamberlain proved generally acceptable to the other members and was supported by them.

What we like to remember in the Commonwealth is the magnificent way in which we all rallied in 1940 to the inspired leadership of Mr. Churchill, how we in the overseas Dominions were the allies of Britain when Europe was overrun, and she had no other allies, "how the British people held the fort ALONE till those who hitherto had been half blind were half ready." We need to remind ourselves today also that in the 1930's the weakness, the vacillation, the appeasement policies of the British government seemed to most of the overseas Commonwealth statesmen the best form of statesmanship available in a very difficult world.[8]

Several features in this unhappy situation of the 1930's are worth recalling. Most important of all was the fundamental weakness of Britain herself, economic and strategic. She had won the war of 1914 at a price which she could not afford, and she was no longer able to play the masterful part in the world which she had played in the nineteenth century. In addition, the British and the other Commonwealth peoples had acquired an abhorrence of war which was almost total. These two facts explain the doubts and the hesitations of the 1930's.

The League of Nations failed to meet the test of the 1930's, and to this failure the British nations were main contributors.[9] All the British governments had insisted during the peaceful 1920's that the League of Nations should not develop, as the

8. For a penetrating analysis of the statesmanship of these years, see Nicholas Mansergh, *Survey of British Commonwealth Affairs: Problems of External Policy, 1931-1939* (London, 1952).

9. On the policies of Commonwealth statesmen concerning the League of Nations, see Gwendolen Carter, *The British Commonwealth and International Security; the Role of the Dominions, 1919-1939* (Toronto, 1947).

French wished, into an international police force. In the words of Prime Minister King of Canada, it was to be an international round table, but not an international war office. The chief Canadian delegate at the League Assembly on one famous occasion had explained that Canada lived in a fireproof house; therefore, she did not feel the need of the insurance which some European countries, closer to possible conflagrations, might wish.

The Canadians had already tried to delete Article X from the Covenant or to get it watered down into noncommittal language. Article X was the clause in the Covenant by which every member guaranteed the territorial integrity and existing political independence of every other member. This had been one of the stumbling blocks which had kept the United States Senate from ratifying the German peace treaty. The Canadian Prime Minister, Sir Robert Borden, had objected to it in Paris in 1919 as strenuously as any American Senator did later on. But membership in the League was a symbol to Canada and to the other Dominions of their newly won international status. The United States did not need any such symbol.

So the Canada which went into the League was, in effect, as isolationist as the America which stayed out, as was to be shown by King's steady policy of no commitments through the successive crises of the 1930's. King was steadily supported by the

bulk of Canadian opinion. He was the great typical Canadian of this generation; he was also the
great typical Commonwealth statesman of the
1920's and 1930's. Thus Canada had the decisive
voice in determining what the Commonwealth
should become. On March 30, 1939, just a few
months before war was to break out, King made
a significant declaration in the Canadian House of
Commons. Referring to certain permanent underlying factors which determine policy he said:

   The first factor is the one that is present and dominant
in the policy of every other country, from Britain and
Sweden to Argentina and the United States. I mean the
existence of a national feeling and the assumption that
first place will be given to the interests, immediate or
long-range, of the country itself. The growth of national
feeling in Canada has been inevitable at a time when
nationalism has come to dominate every quarter of the
world. . . . A strong and dominant national feeling is
not a luxury in Canada, it is a necessity. Without it
the country could not exist. . . .
   In many, but certainly not in all cases this growth of
national feelings has strengthened the desire for a policy
which its defenders call minding one's own business and
which its critics call isolationism. Assuming, it is urged,
that Canadians like other people will put their own interests first, what do our interests demand, what amount of
knight errantry abroad do our resources permit? . . .
We have tremendous tasks to do at home . . . we must,
to a greater or less extent, choose between keeping our
own house in order, and trying to save Europe and Asia.
The idea that every twenty years this country should automatically and as a matter of course take part in a war

overseas for democracy or self-determination of other small nations, that a country which has all it can do to run itself should feel called upon to save, periodically, a continent that cannot run itself, and to these ends risk the lives of its people, risk bankruptcy and political disunion, seems to many a nightmare and sheer madness.

It is to be noted that, with characteristic King caution, the Canadian Prime Minister said that the idea of Canadian armed intervention in Europe every twenty years seemed to many a nightmare and sheer madness. He did not say that it seemed so to Mackenzie King. But all his hearers and readers assumed that this was what he meant. Yet, a few months later, September 10, 1939, King carried his country into the European war without a single vote in Parliament against his action. Canada went into the war, as Britain did under the Chamberlain leadership, only after a long policy of unheroic patience and appeasement had made it clear that there was no other way of curbing Hitler's insatiable ambitions. The important point was, that, for the second time in one generation, she went into a European war at Britain's side.

Away back in 1865, John Alexander Macdonald, introducing the scheme of British North American Confederation to the Canadian legislature, had declared:

One argument . . . has been used against this Confederation, that it is an advance towards independence. Some are apprehensive that the very fact of our forming this union will hasten the time when we shall be severed from the mother country.   I have no apprehension of that kind. . . . The colonies are now in a transition state. Gradually a different colonial system is being developed— and it will become, year by year, less a case of dependence on our part and of overruling protection on the part of the Mother Country, and more a case of a healthy and cordial alliance.   Instead of looking upon us as a merely dependent colony, England will have in us a friendly nation—a subordinate but still a powerful people—to stand by her in North America in peace or in war.[10]

By 1945 Canada and the other Dominions had stood by Britain in two world wars within one generation.   This is the fundamental fact that underlies the Commonwealth relationship.

10. *Parliamentary Debates on the Subject of the Confederation of the British North American Colonies* (Quebec, 1865), pp. 43-44.

3

The Second Commonwealth

THE SECOND Commonwealth is that which is emerging from the Second World War in the second half of the twentieth century, the Commonwealth of the second Elizabethan age. It now includes in its membership not only the young overseas nations peopled mainly by European stock and inheriting a British or, at any rate, a European civilization, but also older nations in Asia: India, Pakistan, and Ceylon—peoples with rich Oriental cultures of their own and with a history that reaches further back into the past than does British history. It seems likely in a measurable future to take in some communities in Africa with colored populations. One of the difficulties facing it will be to decide what are the conditions of eligibility for these new applicants to membership and what authority decides upon their eligibility. If admission to the Commonwealth club is to be by vote of the existing membership, will a majority vote be sufficient, or will one blackball exclude? This is a question on which Great Britain, with its comparatively liberal feelings about color, and South Africa, with its fanatical dedication to white supremacy, are likely to have decidedly different views.

The relations of these newly admitted non-European members with the older members will of necessity not be quite so intimate as the relations of the older members with each other. We shall have to face the question, when British control is removed, of how deeply the superimposed British political, legal, and social institutions have penetrated into these fundamentally non-British communities. The essential institution is political democracy. There will be many more occasions for misunderstanding during the century which began with the admission of India in 1949 than there were during the century which began with Lord Durham's Report in 1839. This experiment in a unique pluralistic, multiracial association of peoples is by all odds the most audacious adventure upon which any Britishers in history have ever embarked. If it fails, if European peoples cannot live together with Asiatics and Africans as equals and as partners within this loose free-and-easy Commonwealth, what chances are there for peace among the peoples of the world in the rest of the twentieth century? But if this experiment, this project of a commonwealth, succeeds, our poets will have cause indeed for celebrating the second Elizabethan age.

The challenge of World War II revealed a remarkably united Commonwealth considering the looseness of its formal bonds, but not a completely united one. By September 3, 1939, each of the various member-states had fully established its right to make its own decision about participation. Ireland had rejected the Dominion status imposed in 1921; as an independent republic, she remained neutral. In South Africa Generals Smuts and Hertzog had agreed at the time of Munich in 1938 on nonbelligerency if war should break out then; a year later the two leaders of the United Party split; and Smuts carried a divided Union Parliament into war, convinced that South Africa could not afford to allow Nazi power to get loose in black Africa. Australia and New Zealand went into the war willingly along with Britain, as in 1914.

Canada took a week to make up her mind, during which, as a neutral, she imported munitions of war from the United States and, as a belligerent, arrested German nationals within her boundaries. On September 10, His Majesty made a separate declaration of war for Canada; and Prime Minister King, who had a Gladstonian capacity for discovering profound moral imperatives behind all his own actions, was soon proclaiming the war as a struggle of the forces of righteousness against the forces of evil.

In India, which as yet had Responsible Government only in its provinces and not at the center in New Delhi, the Viceroy carried the country into war without consulting the native nationalist leaders, an action which caused deep resentment among them and gave them justification for claiming that India could not fight for other peoples' freedom until she was free herself.

This second war was carried on without the setting up of any Imperial War Cabinet. Many leaders in Britain and the Dominions would have liked something of the kind. But King was unalterably opposed; and, as usual in Commonwealth affairs, the Canadian veto was effective. King claimed, with some justice, that there was actually in operation a continuous conference of all the Commonwealth cabinets, made possible by modern communications. The Prime Ministers and their colleagues and officials could all consult their opposite numbers freely by telephone, by cables and wireless messages, and by frequent air-borne visits to each other.

Canada had, by this time, initiated another development in which gradually all the other Dominions copied her. A Canadian Department of External Affairs in Ottawa had been set up only

a few years before World War I; it remained
a small, inconspicuous body down to the end of
that war and played a very humble part in the
peace negotiations. By 1918 there were twenty-
one on the staff. After King became Prime
Minister in the 1920's, he proceeded to build up
the Department under the able headship of Oscar
Douglas Skelton, one of his chief confidential ad-
visers, who had been Professor of Political Science
at Queen's University. Skelton, following the
model of the British Civil Service, staffed his department with a selection of the cream of young
university graduates in economics, political science,
and history; these Canadian eggheads have won
for it during the past thirty years a world-wide
reputation.

In 1920, just before retiring from office, Sir
Robert Borden got the consent of the British and
American governments to a Canadian minister in
Washington. This, it was announced in the best
diplomatic phraseology, would not involve any
breach in the diplomatic unity of the British Empire. For some reason the minister was not appointed till 1927, when King named Mr. Vincent
Massey, the present Governor-General of Canada.
By the time the Canadian minister arrived in
Washington, there was already an Irish minister
there; in 1921 the Irish Free State had come into
existence as a Dominion with all the rights

possessed by the Dominion of Canada, and it had immediately proceeded to exercise one of these rights by appointing an Irish minister to Washington.

In the years between 1927 and 1939 Canadian legations were established in Paris and Tokyo, and a Canadian minister was appointed to serve jointly in Belgium and the Netherlands. There were no Canadian ministers in the centers of trouble that mattered most: in Berlin, Moscow, or Rome. But during the war ministers were sent to several Latin American countries, to Soviet Russia, and to China. Since the war this Canadian diplomatic representation has expanded by leaps and bounds. There are now thirty-seven Canadian embassies or legations in foreign capitals, plus three permanent delegations in NATO, the United Nations at New York, and the United Nations at Geneva, plus seven High Commissioners in the other Commonwealth capitals. The total personnel strength of the Department of External Affairs now amounts to more than fifteen hundred.

This building up of an expert staff in external relations at Ottawa and of diplomatic contacts abroad is one of King's great services to his country. Until Canada had her own agencies for keeping in touch with what was going on in the world, she was dependent for information and for the interpretation of that information upon the

British Foreign Office—or else upon the New York *Times*. Obviously, there was considerable un-reality in speaking of Canada's equality of status, much more so in suggesting any equality of func-tion, under such circumstances.

Of the other Dominions, the Irish Free State and South Africa followed the Canadian example vigorously. Australia and New Zealand disap-proved of it, preferring to build up their sources of information by close liaison inside the British Foreign Office and diplomatic service. But, when Hitler overran western Europe and Japan cut loose in eastern Asia, it became clear that the security of the two South Pacific Dominions depended henceforth on the United States rather than on Britain. Australian and New Zealand ministers then quickly appeared in Washington.

One would judge, incidentally, that the Aus-tralians and New Zealanders hardly speak to Washington with the same uninhibited freedom that we Canadians exercise. While the United States will do its best to protect them, the two South Pacific countries are, if necessary, expend-able. So they watch their manners when in Ameri-can company. Canadians, no matter how we be-have, are not expendable. The United States must defend us to the last. If Canada is ever abandoned to the enemy, it will be on the day before Chicago and Detroit are abandoned. Hence the remarkable freedom and frequency with which our Secretary of State for External Affairs delivers public lectures to the State Department.

By 1945, when the San Francisco conference was held to set up the United Nations, each member-state of the Commonwealth sent its own diplomatic delegation as a matter of course. Nothing could demonstrate more clearly how far things had moved since 1919 than the matter-of-course attitude in which the rest of the world accepted this phenomenon. At San Francisco the talk was not of whether there was a British Commonwealth bloc operating in the meetings, but whether Canada or Australia might try to lead a bloc of middle powers against the claims of the great powers.

There is still a good deal of truth, however, now that all the member states of the Commonwealth have equipped themselves with effective agencies for making their own external policies, in the original statement of 1920, that the diplomatic unity of the Commonwealth has not been thereby destroyed. The Commonwealth High Commissioners in London consult regularly in common meetings with the British Secretary of State for Commonwealth Relations. At Washington the eight Commonwealth ambassadors also meet regularly with each other. On this matter the testimony of Sir Oliver Franks, recently the British Ambassador in Washington, is worth taking.

In Washington I saw how that [Commonwealth] unity worked. Every fortnight except in the summer the eight Ambassadors of the Commonwealth met in our Embassy to exchange views and consult informally together. We discussed everything: the movement of affairs in the world, the latest phase of American policy—and the opinions of our different countries about them. We did not mince words. Even difficulties between individual members, like Kashmir, were regularly talked over by all of us, including India and Pakistan, with conviction but without heat. Further, the discussions took place between like-minded people who shared a common political tradition. No one had to insist on the freedom of his country because nobody ever questioned it. We had forbearance, which is essential between members of a continuing club when they differ.

What did I get out of this experience? A new view of the power and positive influence of the Commonwealth countries in the world. A better conception of what the equality and independence of our partners means to them and to us. I could see that any notion of Britain as a mother with a number of sons, now all legally of age but still a trifle undergraduateish in outlook, is totally mistaken. We are dealing with equals. They expect to be consulted on matters of common interest before we act and not told about it afterwards. If we forget for a moment and act in terms of an older relationship, the reminder that we get is quick and unambiguous.[1]

Let us turn now to another aspect of this modern Commonwealth, the failure of British statesmanship in Ireland and its brilliant success, after seeming during the 1930's to be headed for disastrous failure, in India.

1. Sir Oliver Franks, *Britain and the Tide of World Affairs* (London, 1955).

Englishmen for four centuries have shown themselves at their worst in dealing with Ireland. After generations of bitterness, Gladstone thought he might bring about a reconciliation between the English and Irish. But he was frustrated by the obstinate English insistence that Ireland must remain an integral part of the United Kingdom. When Irish nationalists, the Sinn Feiners, finally succeeded in 1921 in breaking the Union of 1800, they did it by fighting a bloody civil war. In turn, they were compelled by Lloyd George, under the threat of continuing the civil war until Ireland had been reduced by superior British force, to accept "dominion status" in the Commonwealth, which was not what they wanted. This element of force and violence has poisoned Anglo-Irish relations throughout and has prevented the friendly Commonwealth relationship from developing.

In 1921 Irish nationalists, as a price of freedom, had to accept the partition of their island. They also had dominion status imposed upon them. What an irony, or a tragedy, that the position in which Canada was so proudly exulting at this very time should be one which seemed humiliating to Irish patriots. But humiliating it was. They had fought for an Irish republic; they played with the idea of some sort of link with Britain for foreign affairs, which they described as "External

Association." They were forced to accept an oath of allegiance to the British monarch, a monarchical Governor-General, an appeal from their courts to the British Privy Council. British rigidity and lack of imagination, British worship of forms regardless of the reality behind them, forced the Irish to fit themselves willy-nilly into the framework which had been found so satisfactory to Canada.

Even so, as things settled down in the 1920's, and as the Balfour Report of 1926 was followed by the Statute of Westminster of 1931, the British claim that dominion status would be found flexible enough even for Irish nationalism had a chance of being proved true. But there was too much obstinacy on both sides, and there were too many occasions of friction. Mr. de Valera came to office in Dublin and proceeded methodically to get rid of the oath of allegiance, the judicial appeal, and eventually the Governor-General, after subjecting that unhappy monarchial functionary to all the humiliations he could think of. By 1936, when the other Commonwealth states were settling the new succession to the throne on the abdication of King Edward VIII, he was giving his part of Ireland a republican constitution. In 1938 Ireland stayed neutral, and in 1949 she officially left the Commonwealth altogether.

Here is the great failure of British statesmanship in our day. What had become of that British
genius for avoiding definition and for meeting
difficulties with pragmatic *ad hoc* expedients? One
of the strange facts about the Commonwealth
in these years is that Anglo-Irish relations, in spite
of Imperial Conferences and other means of com-
munication, seem to have been mostly conducted
without consulting the other member-states. This
is worth remembering when we hear voluble as-
surances as to continuous consultation. One sus-
pects that in such delicate situations the Commonwealth statesmen tend to avoid unpleasant topics
of discussion, as they are doing at present in the
matter of South Africa's fanatical policy on the
color question.

It looked through the 1930's as if India would
go the way of Ireland as soon as she got a chance;
after the outbreak of war in 1939, it looked as if
India had adopted the Irish motto that England's
difficulties are Ireland's opportunities. Fortu-
nately, British statesmanship or, more precisely,
British Labor statesmanship, learned something
from the Irish failure; in 1949 an Indian republic
became a full member of the Commonwealth.

On August 20, 1917, at the very moment when
the white self-governing colonies were working out
their new Dominion status in the Empire, the
British government—a coalition government that

included the three parties, Liberal, Conservative, and Labor—announced in Parliament a new policy for India. Its policy, said the Secretary of State for India, was "the gradual development of self-governing institutions, with a view to the progressive realisation of responsible government in India as an integral part of the British Empire." Progress in this policy, he added, would be by successive stages; and the time and measure of each advance would be determined by the British and Indian Governments, i.e., *not* by the Indian people and their political leaders.[2]

Twenty painful years followed, full of nationalist agitation and bitterness, of unsuccessful negotiations between Indian leaders and British authorities. In view of the obstinate slowness with which British governments showed themselves disposed to honor the promise of 1917 and of the extreme feelings and actions which frustration inevitably caused among Indian politicians, an outside observer could hardly help concluding that India was about to be lost, as Ireland was being lost. The man at Westminster chiefly responsible for British reluctance to make concessions to Indian nationalism was Mr. Winston Churchill, at the head of a group of die-hard Tories. Nevertheless, whatever criticisms we may make of the short-

2. For the text of this Montagu Declaration, see Arthur Berriedale Keith, *Speeches and Documents on Indian Policy*, II, 133-34.

comings of British statesmanship in these years, we should remember that the Gandhi technique of non-violent non-cooperation, of mass passive resistance, could only have succeeded in embarrassing a government that was fundamentally liberal. How quickly would Gandhi have been liquidated in the Germany or Russia or Japan of his day! Though Mr. Churchill might announce on becoming Prime Minister in 1940 that he did not intend to preside over the liquidation of the British Empire, his government was soon negotiating with the Indian leaders about the terms on which Indian independence could be brought about.

It was left to Mr. Clement Attlee in the postwar Labor government to force the hands of quarreling Hindus and Moslems by setting a date at which Britain would get out of India, by fixing the boundaries of the new states of India and Pakistan, and by leaving the two communities and the Indian native princes to settle for themselves the basis of their future relations. This drastic action by a liberal in the best Durham tradition has had a triumphant success. In 1947 acts were passed in the British Parliament for the independence of India and Pakistan, to come into effect on August 15. Later in the same year, a Ceylon Independence Act was passed.

Note the frank use in these official documents of the word *independence*. In Canada and in the earlier Dominion, we have shrunk from this daring word; we have always substituted the word *autonomy*. *Independence* has too many overtones of 1776; now, apparently, the British Commonwealth is no longer afraid of the memories of that year.

India has used her independence to make herself a republic. Pakistan is in process of doing the same thing. Burma, which became independent at the same time, used her independence to opt for complete departure from the Commonwealth connection. Only little Ceylon decided to remain a monarchical Dominion, owing allegiance to the British Crown like the older Dominions.

In April, 1949, a conference of Commonwealth prime ministers was held in London. Here the Indian Prime Minister presented the decision of his people to establish a sovereign independent republic, declaring at the same time India's "desire to continue her full membership in the Commonwealth of Nations and her acceptance of the King as the symbol of the free association of its independent member nations, and as such the Head of the Commonwealth." On these terms Indian was voted into the club.

Here was the most spectacular event in the constitutional evolution of the modern Commonwealth. A republic is accepted into membership; and while its citizens repudiate allegiance to the King, they recognize the King as the symbol of the free Commonwealth form of association and as the Head of the Commonwealth. We have not been told what were the steps in negotiation by which this conclusion was reached. And, having recovered by 1949 our old British genius for avoiding definition, none of us in the Commonwealth has since inquired too curiously what are the powers and functions of this Head of the Commonwealth.

We continue to show a considerable amount of variety in describing the position. When Queen Elizabeth II succeeded to the throne, she was proclaimed by different titles in different states. In the United Kingdom her present title is: "Elizabeth the Second, by the Grace of God, of the United Kingdom of Great Britain and Northern Ireland, and of Her other Realms and Territories, Queen, Head of the Commonwealth, Defender of the Faith." Canada, Australia, and New Zealand, in their form of title, add their own names after that of the United Kingdom. In South Africa she is "Elizabeth the Second, Queen of South Africa and Her other Realms and Territories, Head of the Commonwealth"; here, instead of being mentioned first, the United Kingdom is merely included without name in "her other Realms and Territories." Similarly, in Ceylon. In Pakistan her title states that she is "Queen of the United Kingdom and of Her other Realms and Territories," but does not mention Pakistan. India, as a republic, has not proclaimed a title for the Queen. What the phrase "Defender of the Faith" means in Canada, a country in which more than 40 per cent of the population are Roman Catholics, I refuse to contemplate. In the United Kingdom it presumably refers to the Protestant faith, though Henry VIII acquired it for defending the Catholic faith. Pakistan, as a Moslem community, and Ceylon, as a Buddhist community, have dropped "Defender of the Faith" from their titles.

Now, having dealt sketchily with some of the significant developments in the individual member-states of this multi-racial Commonwealth, let us consider two difficult points: the bonds which continue to hold the members together and the difficulties which appear to loom up in the future.

We have already noted the bond of the common Crown. This is the topic with which every right-thinking Britisher would start. It is rather difficult to explain to an audience of republicans how strong and real is the feeling of loyalty to the monarch which moves the minds and hearts and imaginations of the citizens of a monarchical community. Your ancestors put all this aside in the eighteenth century. But in British countries, as the twentieth century has advanced, there has been an increasing volume of tribute from all sides to the importance of the Crown as a symbol of the

unity of the Commonwealth.   We like to tell ourselves nowadays, and we are becoming rather too
fond of doing so, that man is not a rational crea-
ture, that he is governed by emotions and sentiments, and that these can be most readily evoked
by myths and symbols.   Moreover, the new
Queen, by her youthfulness and grace, spreads a
charm so potent that it is almost useless to protest against the overworking of the sentiment that
has now come to surround the monarchy as an
institution.   "The Crown," said Mr. Churchill
on her accession, "has become the mysterious link,
indeed I may say the magic link, which unites our
loosely bound but strongly interwoven Commonwealth of Nations, states and races."[3]

Yet I cannot help feeling that if we Britishers
should all wake up tomorrow morning to find
ourselves living in republics, the British Commonwealth would go on exactly as it was going on
yesterday.   And we should soon be rationalizing
the new phenomenon by remarking what cool,
prosaic, matter-of-fact people we Britishers are,
instead of exclaiming what delightfully sentimental
mystics we are.   When I am told, even by Sir
Winston Churchill, that the British monarchy has
something mysterious or indeed magic about it, I
sigh for the return of some of those good English

3. Quoted by Hessel Duncan Hall, "The British Commonwealth
of Nations," *American Political Science Review*, XLVII (Dec.,
1953), 1012.

Whigs who, from the seventeenth century to the nineteenth, put the monarchy in its place. I wonder whether Whiggism has quite died out from our British subconscious minds.

What really holds the British countries together is the presence of common interests and common ideals. If conflicting interests and ideals should ever become too marked, the symbolism of the monarchy would soon turn out to be a very weak bond of union. Watch what happens in South Africa in the next ten years or so. The only danger facing the British monarchy today is that well-meaning enthusiasts will try to puff it up to a much greater importance than it can possibly maintain.

Moreover, in assessing the position of the Crown, we need to add that in Ireland it suggested only bitter memories of misgovernment and civil discord to the Irishmen who are now citizens of the Irish republic. It was not a symbol of Commonwealth unity to them. In Canada, French Canadians are able to regard it with a much cooler detachment than English Canadians. In South Africa the Afrikans-speaking nationalists talk of a republic. And then there are the new Asiatic Commonwealth states. Of them only little Ceylon remains monarchical. We are now in a position in which the more we older members of the Commonwealth insist on trumpeting our loyalty to the

Crown, the more we tend to alienate the newer members by suggesting to them that the Commonwealth has two grades of citizens, the elite monarchists and the second-class republicans. In such circumstances the Crown may become a symbol that divides. Monarchy does not seem likely to be a unifying symbol in the later twentieth century beyond the parts of the Commonwealth that are peopled by British immigrants and their descendants.

Still, when this has been said, it is also true that everyone in the Commonwealth felt a thrill of pride over the pageantry of the coronation of 1953, a pride which was heightened by the comforting reflection that here, at least, is one exclusive possession of our own, which Hollywood and Madison Avenue cannot vulgarize.

Our interests and ideals, however, keep us in the Commonwealth. Every member state makes some profit, material or immaterial, out of the Commonwealth connections. Every member state acquires some additional importance from its Commonwealth membership. Membership, a New Zealand statesman was reported to have said, means "independence plus." When a Canadian diplomat or an Indian diplomat speaks to the world, he is listened to with more attention than he would be if his country stood by itself in isolated independence. South Africa would be left in a position of extreme loneliness in the black African continent but for her Commonwealth associations. To Pakistan and Ceylon the Commonwealth is a counterforce against unceasing Indian pressure. The Colombo Plan helps the Eastern members economically; it also enables the western members to feel, without any real justification, that, even if they have not as much money as the United States, they have more constructive imagination.

Almost equally important is the mere habit of association, with all the ties that it creates over a long period of years. Nothing has more surprised the world—including, I suppose, both Englishmen and Indians—than the fact that Indian nationalists, after spending a century denouncing English imperialism, now quite obviously prefer Englishmen to Americans. They and the English have long lived in close contact with each other. Mr. Nehru will listen to advice from an Englishman or a Canadian which he will not listen to from an American; the reason is that he knows the Englishman or the Canadian will listen more sympathetically to him. It is hard to overestimate the importance of this bond between men who have been in the habit of talking business and politics with each other for a long time in the same club.

Yet the other side of the picture needs to be emphasized too. The Commonwealth now tends to be divided into two groups: a North Atlantic-South

Pacific group and a South Asiatic group. Members of the first group have definitely taken sides in the cold war; they are tied closely in world politics to the United States; they are individually or jointly allied with the United States for certain purposes. However reluctantly, they accept American leadership. Their peoples may be more reluctant than their governments, but they all realize to a greater or less degree that their survival in this dangerous world depends upon their close co-operation with the United States.

The second group deny the major premise of the thinking of the first group. The lessons which they draw from recent history are quite different from those drawn by us in the West. They would prefer to stay uncommitted in the cold war. They are strongly moved by sentiments of anticolonialism. They tend to assume that a power like Communist China must be virtuous because it is Asiatic, and therefore anticolonial, and that the fact that it is also communist and totalitarian is no cause for suspicion. If Pakistan and Ceylon are beginning to break out of this circle, it is not because they love America more, but because they love India less. Mr. Nehru's India still dreams of an Asiatic Monroe Doctrine, which would leave India and Asia free from Western interference. All this puts an obvious strain upon Commonwealth unity, and we cannot yet see what the outcome may be.

Accentuating this division, and partly cutting across it, is another ugly conflict of policy over the racial and color discrimination being enforced by the present nationalist government in South Africa. Apartheid is a direct negation of the ideals professed by the other members of the Commonwealth. India has carried her protest against racial segregation in South Africa to the United Nations. And we now have the distressing spectacle of some members of the Commonwealth in the Arab-Asian bloc openly attacking another member before a world body, while Britain and the white dominions maintain an embarrassed aloofness. Clearly, the policy of the Arab-Asian bloc is only likely to stiffen South Africa in her stand, and South Africa has a good legal case in maintaining that the United Nations has no right to interfere with her domestic affairs. But one would feel much happier in criticizing India for advertising these intra-Commonwealth differences abroad if there were any evidence that the members of the conference of Commonwealth Prime Ministers were seriously facing up to this problem.

Before the Asiatic members there looms another question which we cannot avoid asking. How deeply has Western democracy sunk into their consciousness? The present elite group of leaders in

India and Pakistan were trained in an English way of life, a good many of them at English schools and universities. They learned English methods of political debate and party organization, English standards of administration in a great civil service headed by English officials, English military organization in the armed services where they served alongside of English officers. What will happen when this generation of leaders dies and a native leadership emerges from that mass democracy of peasants and townsmen who will no longer even be learning the English language? It is hard to believe that the present British orientation of Indian thought and policy will continue to be so powerful.

And behind all other questions lurks the great Asiatic problem. Which country will provide the future leadership of Asia: India or China? Which system can more successfully carry through the necessary social revolution? Can Indian statesmen, relying upon British democratic methods of free discussion and free elections, succeed in bringing about the good life for several hundred million poverty-stricken citizens as rapidly as can the Chinese leaders with their more ruthless methods, inspired by the fanatical drive of Communism? Upon the answer to this question will depend the future of the British Commonwealth in Asia and perhaps in Africa also.

In this field we in North America can only speculate as distant, badly informed observers. Let us, therefore, turn to a field about which we have more information, if not stronger opinions: the North Atlantic triangle of Britain, Canada, and the United States. Britain and Canada may be said almost to favor two opposed interpretations of the Commonwealth, and their tendency to differ derives to a considerable extent from their differing interpretation of the relations of the United States with it.

Most of the writing about the Commonwealth is done by authors in Britain, and most of the insistence that it has some special function or mission in the world comes from these writers. In their hymns of praise one can easily detect a note of anxiety. The number of them who are constantly on mission tours through one part of the Commonwealth or another is also significant. For the British have special reasons for concern about the future; and wishful thinking tempts them to see the Commonwealth through very rosy spectacles. Britain, the original center and heart of the Empire-Commonwealth, has suffered more from the wars and revolutions of our day than has any of its outlying members. She has irrevocably lost the position of the leading world power, which she enjoyed without challenge from 1815 to 1914, and to her the Commonwealth represents her last chance to function as a great power. Or, to speak more precisely, the Commonwealth offers the British governing classes their last chance to play a great part on the world stage. Modern technological developments have brought it about that Britain, by herself, is once again just an island off the north coast of France.

It is primarily the British governing classes who are aware of these profound changes in the position of their country and of the challenge which they face. The British mass-democracy of the twentieth century, now that the century is half over, impresses one as not being greatly interested in the Imperial position of the country. At the close of the nineteenth century, liberals in England were worrying that the masses were going to be corrupted by empire; today those masses seem to be abandoning their empire in a fit of absence of mind. When Mr. Attlee suddenly announced the British retirement from India, this epoch-making action was received by the British public with a remarkable apathy. Not a cock crowed. And later, when the Conservative government had to abandon the British hold on the Suez Canal, the attempt of the tory die-hard wing of the party to work up an emotional storm over this imperial betrayal was a dismal flop. In the modern social welfare state, the British Empire is not for the masses the great system of outdoor relief which a liberal critic declared it to be for the governing classes in the nineteenth century. Sometimes one wonders whether the British public as a whole would not be happier to live in another Sweden, the excitement and the adventure, the glory and the tragedy of empire put behind them.

But this fate will not willingly be accepted by British political leaders of either party. And we had probably better not delude ourselves into thinking that the British are about to settle down to the placid existence of an unambitious, self-centered, equalitarian social-democracy. They are not a nation of shopkeepers, though various enemies have made this mistake about them from century to century. The tradition of greatness is in their blood. It was not a utilitarian, profit-and-loss people who acquired sovereignty over a quarter of the earth's surface. The English have always been a passionate people, and their deepest passion has been that for power.

"There are some," said Sir Oliver Franks last year in his lecture over the B.B.C., "who suggest that the future of Britain lies in making a break with the past and giving up the tradition of greatness. The thing to do is to withdraw from world affairs and lead a quiet life on our island, democratic, contented and reasonably industrious. This is impossible. Geography and history alike forbid it. For us there is no middle way. Nor do most of us really think there is, except in the world of make-believe. This is obvious from our behaviour in times of crisis. We expect to have a say about our destiny and are not prepared to leave it to be decided by others. We assume we have influence and power among the nations."[4]

But the policies which Sir Oliver Franks recommends to his countrymen are not those which they seem disposed to follow. Apparently, the idea which is most congenial to them is that the fostering of the Commonwealth into a closely knit and largely exclusive association is the best way by which they can assure themselves of living in the style to which they have been accustomed. When they are invited to strike out on another line of adventure and to throw themselves into the project of a Western European union, they shy away from it. British spokesmen always give as one of their main reasons for refusing integration with the European continent that their Commonwealth partners object to such a policy and that it would undermine their Commonwealth connections. But they have never quoted a leader from the rest of the Commonwealth to this effect. It is they who invite the Commonwealth to press them to stay out of European commitments, not the other Commonwealth nations who are doing the pressing

4. Sir Oliver Franks, *Britain and the Tide of World Affairs*, p. 2.

spontaneously because of their concern for Commonwealth unity.

This special British solicitude for Commonwealth ties has also an economic basis. Their economy, since the days when they rejected Joseph Chamberlain's proposals in 1905, has become more and more dependent on the Empire. Economically, the British Empire now takes for them the form of the sterling bloc—of which, of course, the second ranking nation in the Commonwealth, Canada, is not a member, for the Canadian economy has moved, since 1914, steadily away from dependence upon Empire connections and towards integration with that of the United States. Evidently, at present British leaders are under a strong temptation to retire from hard competition with Americans and Germans and Japanese in world markets and to seek their economic future inside a closely organized sterling bloc. But this is a policy based on weakness. It is an attempted escape from the responsibilities of greatness. And some British thinkers see clearly enough—Sir Oliver Franks, e.g.—that Britain cannot achieve her political aims of recovering her position as a great world power except on a basis of economic strength. Whether the present Conservative leaders are sufficiently convinced of this may be doubted, and the doubt becomes deeper when one looks at the Labor leaders.

During this last generation the buffetings of fate, political and economic, have combined to tempt the British towards seeking their salvation inside a closed Commonwealth. But here there is another challenge facing them, of which even the wisest of them hardly seem sufficiently conscious. Because she has been the accepted leader of the Empire-Commonwealth for so long, Britain tends to assume that she can continue to take this position of leadership for granted. She is suffering from what Toynbee calls the nemesis of creativity. But the hard fact is that her position of leadership has now to be earned anew by her every day. There is no example in history of a group of states cohering voluntarily over a long period without effective leadership from one of them. Now, to put it mildly, the failure of the British economy to recover a secure position in the world since the war and the conduct of British diplomacy in certain quarters of the world are not encouraging. The way in which the British have handled Iran, Egypt, Cyprus, Kenya, does not provide much evidence for the supposed British possession of a special know-how not vouchsafed to North Americans. In fairness, one must balance against these items the British success at home in achieving the social-welfare state without bitter class conflict, their imaginative experiments in such dependencies as Nigeria and the Gold Coast, and their skill in maintaining good relations with India. But the challenge which faces Britain today is a harder one than she has faced for centuries, always presuming that she is determined to remain a great power.

It is also a more complex challenge. For the British Commonwealth as a unit can no longer be successfully defended by its own power, no matter how it is organized. This is the fundamental change which has taken place since 1914. In most of the Commonwealth countries the governments, more realistic than their peoples, have adjusted themselves to this challenge by entering, jointly and individually, into new alliances with the United States. In the Western World, for as long as we can foresee, the United States has supplanted Britain as leader. And this makes unreal all aspirations for a closed exclusive British Commonwealth, economic or political.[5]

Canada is the member of the Commonwealth that has carried furthest the tendency to develop contacts and commitments outside the Commonwealth.[6] However much old-fashioned Canadian

5. "The ultimate, though not the intended, effect of United States diplomacy may be to promote the security of the individual members of the Commonwealth at the expense of the unity of the Commonwealth as a whole." This was suggested by an Indian paper at the Lahore conference. Nicholas Mansergh, *The Multi-Racial Commonwealth* (London, 1954), p. 44.

6. Canada also took the initiative in 1946 in establishing Canadian citizenship as the primary status of a Canadian, with the status of British subject or Commonwealth citizen relegated to a secondary, derivative position. The other members of the Com-

loyalists may protest, our primary Canadian commitments are now outside the Commonwealth. Our chief Canadian problem is that of adjusting our sentiments and emotions to the practical policies which the world situation has forced on us. Canadian policy, as a matter of fact, has always been oriented towards the North Atlantic rather than towards the British Empire. Our security has depended upon good relations between Britain and the United States. In the North Atlantic triangle our fundamental policy has consisted in balancing the British connection against American pressures. Though we have talked a great deal about the Empire, and still do, you can nearly always get the real practical meaning of our talk if for the word *Empire* you substitute the word *Britain*. Our attention has been concentrated in the North Atlantic. Till very recently we have never known or cared much about the parts of the British Empire scattered over the seven seas, and we still have very few contacts with them. In this present generation Canadian armed forces crossed the Atlantic twice, on each occasion to save Britain. The Empire was a secondary consideration.

As soon as it became clear in 1940 that the Grand Alliance of Britain and France and their associates could not defend Europe against Hitler

---

monwealth have followed the Canadian example, but in Britain this was done with considerable publicly expressed reluctance.

by themselves and that the whole basis of Canadian security had been changed, Canada set up a permanent joint defense board with the United States to lay plans for the security of the North American continent. Today the two North American neighbors have entered upon the ambitious co-operative schemes of the three radar lines across Canada to defend them against aggression from another enemy, who is Canada's neighbor in the Arctic. When Soviet aggression in Europe became dangerous, Canada and the United States helped to form the North Atlantic Treaty Organization with the Western European powers, and today Canada is keeping Canadian armed forces in Western Europe in a time of peace, a revolution in her policy that would have been inconceivable to the Canadians of the 1930's. Who would have believed then that the Canada which had always steadfastly refused to make definite, specific defense commitments to Britain would, in another twenty years, have committed herself in this startling way to an alliance of which the United States was to be the acknowledged leader?

Certainly, the Canadian people feel a vague uneasiness about this revolution of 1940, which has so completely reoriented their external policies. They are aware that they spent one hundred years, from 1839 to 1939, in achieving their independence from Great Britain; and they wonder whether they will have to spend the hundred years from the Ogdensburg agreement of 1940 in maintaining their independence against the United States. Some of them fear that the United States is already building up an empire over them in a fit of absence of mind. But no Canadian who is realistic about the problems of his country sees any possibility of withdrawing from these American commitments; and it is useless to stick our heads in the sand and to pretend that the diplomatic unity of the British Commonwealth is still what it was before 1940.

Incidentally, it should be noted, as showing once more how completely Canadian policy is preoccupied with the North Atlantic, that though a minute Canadian force served in the Korean war, Canada has declined to join in the South-East Asia Treaty Organization, in spite of the fact that Britain, Australia, New Zealand, and Pakistan are members. As for our contribution to the Colombo Plan, which is always trotted out in argument by the proponents of a British Commonwealth united front, our Canadian twenty-five million dollars a year is equivalent to the silver contribution the prosperous churchman puts in the collection plate every Sunday morning while his mind is preoccupied with his more important weekday concerns.

In proportion to her total economic, political, and military activity, Canada is more closely connected with the United States than is any other member of the Commonwealth. At the opposite extreme is India, which shuns the defilement of American contacts. In between, nearly all the other members have American commitments of some kind. Australia and New Zealand, when they joined in the ANZUS pact with the United States, offended Britain by agreeing with the Americans in refusing to admit her. Pakistan receives arms from the United States, which may be for protection against Communist power or against Indian power. And Britain herself has not merely the obligation of membership in NATO and SEATO, but has been compelled to transfer to the Americans her burdens in Greece and Turkey, to look for American help in getting out of the mess in Iran, and to maneuver warily in Israel and Egypt with the State Department breathing down her neck. In the United Nations and in Big Four meetings in Geneva, British and American policies have to be carefully co-ordinated in advance, or they frustrate each other. Wherever we look today, something new has been added to the British Commonwealth, something American. All roads in the Commonwealth lead to Washington.[7]

7. An interesting little example of the penetration of American influences into the innermost circles of the British faithful is the fact, mentioned by Professor Mansergh in his report of the unofficial British Commonwealth Relations Conference at Lahore in 1954 (*The Multi-Racial Commonwealth*), that the various national institutes of International Affairs in the Commonwealth

Well, what is the conclusion from all this? What is the future of the British peoples and of their Commonwealth? Some twenty years ago a very shrewd Britisher, the late Sir Fred Clarke, who had lived in South Africa and Canada as well as in Britain, wrote an article which deserves to be better remembered than it has been, if only for its most suggestive title. He called it " 'British' with a Small 'b.' "[8] Like all his countrymen in the 1930's, Clarke was concerned about the declinging power of Britain, her seeming incapacity for decisive action. He suggested, however, that as her power declined, her influence might expand, if she continued to cherish those values which he called British with a small *b*. The purely local tribal institutions, which he called British with a capital *B*, would be such things, I suppose, as the monarchy (or, at any rate, the monarchy that has something mysterious or magical about it), the peerage, the Church of England, the old school tie, the Oxford-B.B.C. accent, "Brittania rules the waves," a certain condescension towards foreigners. British with a small *b* are the long tradition of the freedom and dignity of the individual,

were able to strengthen their delegations to Lahore through financial assistance given to them by the Carnegie Corporation of New York. The Canadian Institute of International Affairs finances some of its publication activities with the aid of grants from the Carnegie Corporation.

8. Sir Fred Clarke, " 'British' with a Small 'b,' " *Nineteenth Century*, CXIX (April, 1936), 428-39.

the habit of reaching decisions by discussion, the spirit of toleration, the flair for compromise, a sense of limits, social solidarity, the independence of the judiciary, a free press, free political parties, free churches, free trade unions. But these, as Clarke pointed out, are precisely the features of British civilization that have a universal appeal. It is the men and women who are British with a small *b*, whatever their race or color, who have turned the Empire into the Commonwealth.

Now, the rest of the world is apprehensive about certain institutions and people in the United States, which it regards as American with a capital *A*, about the "American Century," about "Private Enterprise" (in quotation marks), about—but I am your guest and had better watch my manners. I shall not present you with a list of those individuals whom we outsiders consider to be American with a capital *A*. Let me say that there are many more people scattered through these forty-eight states who are American with a small *a* than outsiders are always ready to admit, and that they are to be found in specially large numbers in American universities. The future of the Western World depends upon the wholeheartedness with which all those people scattered throughout the Commonwealth who are British with a small *b* get together with all those people in the United States who are American with a small *a*.

4

Readings on the History of the British Empire-Commonwealth Since 1839

THIS LIST includes some short narrative histories, but it is mainly based on the assumption that the general reader will understand better the problems of the Empire-Commonwealth if he refers to writings that discuss ideas and policies rather than to those that devote themselves to a detailed narrative of events.

I. *General Histories*

CARRINGTON, CHARLES EDMUND. *The British Overseas: Exploits of a Nation of Shopkeepers.* Cambridge, 1950.

EGERTON, HUGH EDWARD. *A Short History of British Colonial Policy, 1606-1909.* 12th ed., revised by Arthur Percival Newton. London, 1950.

KNAPLUND, PAUL. *The British Empire, 1815-1939.* New York, 1941.

SCHUYLER, ROBERT LIVINGSTON. *The Fall of the Old Colonial System: A Study in British Free Trade, 1770-1870.* New York, 1945.

TYLER, JOHN ECCLESFIELD. *The Struggle for Imperial Unity, 1868-1895.* London, 1938.

WALKER, ERIC ANDERSON. *The British Empire, Its Structure and Spirit, 1497-1953.* 2nd ed., Cambridge, 1954.

WILLCOX, WILLIAM BRADFORD. *Star of Empire: A Study of Britain as a World Power, 1485-1945.* New York, 1950.

Any selection from the great number of histories of the Empire is likely to be somewhat arbitrary. Of all the general single-volume histories, Walker seems to have the best balance between a narrative of events and the interpretation of ideas. Knaplund is among the best of the type that is packed with detailed facts. Egerton was an imperialist of the generation before 1914; his discussion of policy shows this bias. Carrington presents the British as they would like to see themselves in their more romantic moments. Willcox's analysis is that of an understanding American. Schuyler, one of the chief American authorities on the history of the Empire, analyzes the decline of imperialism which culminated in the Manchester School; Tyler follows with the new imperialism of the late Victorian period.

II. *Collections of Documents*

KEITH, ARTHUR BERRIEDALE, ed. *Selected Speeches and Documents on British Colonial Policy, 1763-1917.* (World's Classics). 2 vols. London, 1948; first published, 1918.

KEITH, ARTHUR BERRIEDALE, ed. *Speeches and Documents on the British Dominions, 1918-1931.* (World's Classics). London, 1932.

KEITH, ARTHUR BERRIEDALE, ed. *Speeches and Documents on Indian Policy, 1750-1921.* (World's Classics). 2 vols. London, 1922.

KEITH, ARTHUR BERRIEDALE, ed. *Speeches and Documents on International Affairs, 1918-1937.* (World's Classics). 2 vols. London, 1938.

MANSERGH, NICHOLAS, ed. *Documents and Speeches on British Commonwealth Affairs, 1931-1952.* 2 vols. London, 1953.

In the twenty-five years after 1914 Professor Keith published successive volumes of scholarly analysis of British Commonwealth affairs, which were standard books in their time; they are still worth consulting. The little volumes of documents in the World's Classics series illustrate the background of the events of the 1920's and 1930's. Professor Mansergh's two massive volumes, over 1300 pages, give a fuller coverage to the period since 1931.

III. *The Commonwealth since* 1917

HANCOCK, WILLIAM KEITH. *Survey of British Commonwealth Affairs.* Vol. I, *Problems of Nationality, 1918-1936;* Vol. II, *Problems of Economic Policy, 1918-1939.* London, 1937, 1942.

MANSERGH, NICHOLAS. *Survey of British Commonwealth Affairs: Problems of External Policy, 1931-1939.* London, 1952.

It is almost impossible to overpraise these two great works, which are the standard studies of the modern Commonwealth. Mansergh promises another volume on the period since 1939. Hancock is an Australian by birth; Mansergh, an Irishman; their work is evidence that creative writing on the Commonwealth as well as its creative statesmanship tends to come from the periphery rather than from the center.

BAILEY, SYDNEY DAWSON, ed. *Parliamentary Government in the Commonwealth, A Symposium*. London, 1951.

BRADY, ALEXANDER. *Democracy in the Dominions: A Comparative Study in Institutions*. 2d ed., Toronto, 1952.

CARTER, GWENDOLEN MARGARET. *The British Commonwealth and International Security: The Role of the Dominions, 1919-1939*. (Canadian Institute of International Affairs. Studies in International Affairs, no. 2). Toronto, 1947.

HARVEY, HEATHER JOAN. *Consultation and Cooperation in the Commonwealth: A Handbook on Methods and Practice*. Oxford, 1952.

JENNINGS, SIR WILLIAM IVOR. *The British Commonwealth of Nations*. London, 1948.

JENNINGS, SIR WILLIAM IVOR, AND YOUNG, C. M. *Constitutional Laws of the Commonwealth*. Oxford, 1952.

KEITH, ARTHUR BERRIEDALE. *Responsible Government in the Dominions*. 2 vols. 2d ed., London, 1928. The standard work covering constitutional developments in the Empire-Commonwealth down to the end of the 1920's.

MANSERGH, NICHOLAS. *The Commonwealth and the Nations: Studies in British Commonwealth Relations*. London, 1948.

MANSERGH, NICHOLAS. *The Multi-Racial Commonwealth*. London, 1955. An analysis of the discussion at the unofficial Commonwealth Relations Conference at Lahore, 1954.

WHEARE, KENNETH CLINTON. *The Statute of West-minster and Dominion Status.* 5th ed., London, 1953.

IV. *Biographies, Memoirs, and Biographical Studies*

Short histories are likely to give the impression of an inevitable, predetermined evolution. This impression may be corrected by reading biographies of men who strove to achieve or to prevent certain results, but who did not know what the future would be. There is room here for only a selected list of biographies and memoirs. Biographies of two figures of primary importance in the history of the Commonwealth are promised shortly, that of William Lyon Mackenzie King by Professor Robert MacGregor Dawson and that of Field Marshal Smuts by Sir Keith Hancock.

AMERY, LEOPOLD CHARLES MAURICE STENNETT. *My Political Life.* 3 vols. London, 1953-1955. Unfortunately, Mr. Amery did not live to bring his memoirs beyond 1939. They contain a Chamberlainite interpretation of British history and provide the most fascinating of all recent writing on British politics except that of Sir Winston Churchill.

ANDREWS, CHARLES FREER. *Mahatma Gandhi, His Own Story.* London, 1930.

BLAKE, ROBERT. *The Unknown Prime Minister: The Life and Times of Bonar Law.* London, 1955.

BORDEN, SIR ROBERT LAIRD. *Robert Laird Borden: His Memoirs,* ed. by Henry Borden. 2 vols., Toronto, 1938.

BUCHAN, JOHN. *Lord Minto, A Memoir*. London, 1924.

BUXTON, SYDNEY CHARLES. *General Botha*. London, 1924.

CHURCHILL, SIR WINSTON SPENCER. *The Aftermath*. New York, 1929.

CHURCHILL, SIR WINSTON SPENCER. *Great Contemporaries*. London, 1948.

CHURCHILL, SIR WINSTON SPENCER. *The Second World War*. 6 vols. London, 1948-1954.

CHURCHILL, SIR WINSTON SPENCER. *The World Crisis*. 4 vols. London, 1923, 1927, 1929, 1931; abridged in one volume, 1942.

CRANKSHAW, EDWARD. *The Forsaken Idea: A Study of Viscount Milner*. London, 1952.

CREIGHTON, DONALD GRANT. *John A. Macdonald*. 2 vols. Toronto, 1952-1955.

DRUMMOND, JAMES. *Richard John Seddon*. London, 1907.

DUGDALE, BLANCHE ELISABETH CAMPBELL (BALFOUR). *Arthur James Balfour, First Earl of Balfour*. 2 vols. London, 1936.

DUNCAN, RONALD, ed. *Selected Writings of Mahatma Gandhi*. London, 1951.

FEILING, KEITH GRAHAM. *The Life of Neville Chamberlain*. London, 1947.

FISCHER, LOUIS. *The Life of Mahatma Gandhi*. New York, 1950.

GARVIN, JAMES LOUIS, AND AMERY, JULIAN. *The Life of Joseph Chamberlain*. 4 vols. London, 1932-1951. A fifth volume on Chamberlain's last years is still to come.

GWYNN, DENIS ROLLESTON. *The Life of John Redmond*. London, 1932.

HALPERIN, VLADIMIR. *Lord Milner and the Empire: The Evolution of British Imperialism*. London, 1952.

HAMMOND, JOHN LAWRENCE LE BRETON. *Gladstone and the Irish Nation*. London, 1938.

HARDINGE, SIR ARTHUR HENRY. *The Life of Henry Howard Molyneux Herbert, Fourth Earl of Carnarvon, 1831-1890*. 3 vols. London, 1925.

HEWINS, WILLIAM ALBERT SAMUEL. *The Apologia of an Imperialist: Forty Years of Empire Policy*. 2 vols. London, 1929. Professor Hewins was a leading member of Joseph Chamberlain's brain trust.

HOARE, SAMUEL JOHN GURNEY, VISCOUNT TEMPLEWOOD. *Nine Troubled Years*. London, 1954.

JONES, THOMAS. *Lloyd George*. Cambridge, Mass., 1951.

KNAPLUND, PAUL. *Gladstone and Britain's Imperial Policy*. London, 1927.

KNAPLUND, PAUL. *James Stephen and the British Colonial System*. Madison, 1953.

LLOYD GEORGE, DAVID. *The Truth About the Peace Treaties*. 2 vols. London, 1938.

LLOYD GEORGE, DAVID. *War Memoirs*. 6 vols. London, 1933-1936.

MILLIN, SARAH GERTRUDE. *Cecil Rhodes*. London, 1933.

MORISON, JOHN LYLE. *The Eighth Earl of Elgin: A Chapter in Nineteenth Century Imperial History*. London, 1928.

MURDOCH, WALTER. *Alfred Deakin*. London, 1923.

NEHRU, JAWAHARLAL. *Jawaharlal Nehru, an Autobiography; With Musings on Recent Events in India*. London, 1941.

NEW, CHESTER WILLIAM. *Lord Durham: A Biography of John George Lambton, 1st Earl of Durham*. Oxford, 1929.

NICOLSON, HAROLD GEORGE. *King George the Fifth; His Life and Reign*. London, 1952.

SKELTON, OSCAR DOUGLAS. *Life and Letters of Sir Wilfrid Laurier*. 2 vols. Toronto, 1921.

Smuts, Jan Christiaan. *Jan Christiaan Smuts: A Biography*. London, 1952.

Somervell, David Churchill. *Disraeli and Gladstone*. London, 1932.

Van den Heever, Christiaan Maurits. *General J. B. M. Hertzog*. Johannesburg, 1946.

White, Terence de Vere. *Kevin O'Higgins*. London, 1948.

Williams, Basil. *Botha, Smuts and South Africa*. London, 1946.

Williams, Basil. *Cecil Rhodes*. London, 1938.

Wrong, Edward Murray. *Charles Buller and Responsible Government*. Oxford, 1926.

Zetland, Lawrence John (Lord Ronaldshay). *The Life of Lord Curzon*. 3 vols. London, 1938.

V. *Books of Opinion in Britain*

To understand the interplay of ideas and interests out of which the Commonwealth developed, books of opinion, often very one-sided opinion, may be more revealing than political, constitutional, or diplomatic histories. In this section are listed some of the more important books that contributed to the continuous discussion about the nature of the Empire-Commonwealth, a discussion that is still going on. Some of these books were influential in making opinion in their day; others are included because they expressed so clearly particular points of view.

Amery, Leopold Charles Maurice Stennett, ed. *A Plan of Action; Embodying a Series of Reports Issued by the Research Committee of the Empire Economic Union and other Papers*. London, 1932. Mr.

Amery tells us that his *Plan of Action* was studied by all the delegates at the Ottawa Conference in 1932; if so, they proved poor pupils.

AMERY, LEOPOLD CHARLES MAURICE STENNETT. *The Forward View*. London, 1935.

BENNETT, GEORGE, ed. *The Concept of Empire: Burke to Attlee, 1774-1947*. London, 1953. A collection of some of the most famous and significant statements.

BODELSEN, CARL ADOLF GOTTLIEB. *Studies in Mid-Victorian Imperialism*. New York, 1925.

BULLER, CHARLES. *Responsible Government for Colonies*. London, 1840. Reprinted in Edward Murray Wrong, *Charles Buller and Responsible Government*. Oxford, 1926.

COATMAN, JOHN. *The British Family of Nations*. London, 1950.

COATMAN, JOHN. *Magna Britannia*. London, 1936.

COUPLAND, SIR REGINALD, ed. *The Durham Report*. Oxford, 1945.

COUPLAND, SIR REGINALD. *The Empire in These Days: An Interpretation*. London, 1935.

CURTIS, LIONEL. *The Problem of the Commonwealth*. London, 1916.

DILKE, SIR CHARLES WENTWORTH. *Greater Britain. A Record of Travel in English-Speaking Countries during 1866-67*. London, 1869. A considerable part of this little book is devoted to descriptions of the United States.

DILKE, SIR CHARLES WENTWORTH. *Problems of Greater Britain*. 2 vols. London, 1890. By this time Greater Britain has shrunk to the British Empire.

DUTT, RAJANI PALME. *The Crisis of Britain and the British Empire*. London, 1953.

FRANKS, SIR OLIVER SHEWELL. *Britain and the Tide of World Affairs*. London, 1955. The Reith lectures given in 1954 over the B.B.C.; one of the really great little books of our day.

FROUDE, JAMES ANTHONY. *Oceana; Or, England and Her Colonies.* London, 1886.

GRIGG, SIR EDWARD WILLIAM MACLEAY. *The British Commonwealth: Its Place in the Service of the World.* London, 1944.

HALL, HESSEL DUNCAN. *The British Commonwealth of Nations: A Study of its Past and Future Development.* London, 1920. Jebb's *Britannic Question* presents Chamberlainism as a liberal proposal for "mutual aid in living" in opposition to conservative proposals, such as that of Curtis, for political centralization in a federal system. Hall sets out the Borden-Smuts concept, which supplanted both Chamberlainism and Curtisism.

HANCOCK, SIR WILLIAM KEITH. *Empire in the Changing World* (Penguin Books). New York, 1943.

HINDEN, RITA. *Empire and After: A Study of British Imperial Attitudes.* London, 1949. The Fabian point of view.

HOBHOUSE, LEONARD TRELAWNEY. *Democracy and Reaction.* London, 1904.

HOBSON, JOHN ATKINSON. *Imperialism, A Study.* 5th ed., revised, London, 1952. This book provided an anti-imperialist line of analysis to Lenin as well as to British liberals.

JEBB, RICHARD. *The Britannic Question: A Survey of Alternatives.* London, 1913.

JEBB, RICHARD. *The Empire in Eclipse.* London, 1926.

KEITH, ARTHUR BERRIEDALE. *Imperial Unity and the Dominions.* Oxford, 1916. This book contains some incisive criticism of all proposals for closer integration.

LUCAS, SIR CHARLES P., ed. *Lord Durham's Report on the Affairs of British North America.* 3 vols. Oxford, 1912. Sir Reginald Coupland's abridgement is recommended to readers not interested in too much detail about the Canadas of the 1830's.

MILL, JOHN STUART. "Representative Government," chapter xviii *Of the Government of Dependencies by a Free State*. London, 1861.

PARKIN, SIR GEORGE ROBERT. *Imperial Federation: The Problem of National Unity*. London, 1892.

SEELEY, SIR JOHN ROBERT. *The Expansion of England*. London, 1883.

SMITH, GOLDWIN. *The Empire: A Series of Letters Published in the "Daily News," 1862, 1863*. Oxford, 1863. The pure milk of Manchester doctrine.

WAKEFIELD, EDWARD GIBBON, ed. *A View of the Art of Colonization*. London, 1849.

VI. *Books of Opinion in Canada*

The development of each of the states of the Commonwealth has produced a great deal of writing through the years about that member's future destiny and the nature of its connection with the Empire-Commonwealth. Since Canada has been frequently referred to in these lectures, a selective list of such writings on Canada is given here. Some of these books are by English or other visitors from outside. A similar list could be made for each of the other members of the Commonwealth.

BORDEN, SIR ROBERT LAIRD. *Canada in the Commonwealth, From Conflict to Co-operation*. Oxford, 1929.

BOURASSA, HENRI. *Great Britain and Canada: Topics of the Day*. Montreal, 1902.

BOURASSA, HENRI. *Hier, Aujourd'hui, Demain: Problèmes Nationaux*. Montreal, 1916.

BOURASSA, HENRI. *Independence or Imperial Partnership? A Study of the "Problems of the Commonwealth."* Montreal, 1916. A commentary on Lionel Curtis's *Problem of the Commonwealth.* London, 1916.

BOURASSA, HENRI. *Que Devons-Nous a l'Angleterre? La Défense Nationale: la Révolution Impérialiste: le Tribut à l-Empire.* Montreal, 1915.

These are a few of the many pamphlets in which Bourassa gave expression to French-Canadian anti-imperalist nationalism.

BRYCE, JAMES. *Modern Democracies.* 2 vols. New York, 1921. The section on Canada is based on Bryce's prewar observations while he was ambassador in Washington.

CHAMBERLAIN, WILLIAM HENRY. *Canada, Today and Tomorrow.* Boston, 1942.

CORBETT, PERCY ELLWOOD, AND SMITH, HERBERT ARTHUR. *Canada and World Politics: A Study of the Constitutional and International Relations of the British Empire.* Toronto, 1928.

DAFOE, JOHN WESLEY. *Canada, an American Nation.* New York, 1935.

DENISON, COL. GEORGE TAYLOR. *The Struggle for Imperial Unity: Recollections and Experiences.* London, 1909.

DILKE, SIR CHARLES WENTWORTH. *Problems of Greater Britain.* London, 1890. This book has a long section on Canada, based on Dilke's personal observations; he reaches conclusions different from those of Goldwin Smith.

DOUGHTY, SIR ARTHUR G., ed. *The Elgin-Grey Papers, 1846-1851.* 4 vols. Ottawa, 1937. James Bruce, Earl of Elgin, was Governor-General and Grey Colonial Secretary in the critical years when Responsible Government was established. These Papers contain their private correspondence.

EWART, JOHN SKIRVING. *Kingdom Papers*. Ottawa, 1911-1917. Canadian nationalism as expounded by a constitutional lawyer.

HOBSON, JOHN ATKINSON. *Canada Today*. London, 1906.

KIEWIET, CORNELIUS WILLIAM DE, AND UNDER-HILL, FRANK H., eds. *Dufferin-Carnarvon Correspondence 1874-1878*. Toronto, 1955. The private letters that passed between Lord Dufferin, the Governor-General, and Lord Carnarvon, the Colonial Secretary, in these years.

MACCORMAC, JOHN. *Canada: America's Problem.* New York, 1940.

MILLER, JOHN ORMSBY, ed. *The New Era in Canada; Essays Dealing with the Upbuilding of the Canadian Commonwealth*. New York, 1917.

MORTON, WILLIAM LEWIS, ed. *The Voice of Dafoe; A Selection of Editorials on Collective Security, 1931-1944*. Toronto, 1945. Dafoe was editor of the liberal *Winnipeg Free Press* and the most influential Canadian journalist of his day.

PARKIN, SIR GEORGE ROBERT. *Imperial Federation: The Problem of National Unity*. London, 1892. Denison and Parkin were two Canadians who opposed Smith's ideas.

RUSSELL, SIR WILLIAM HOWARD. *Canada: Its Defences, Condition and Resources*. London, 1865. Russell was the famous *Times* war correspondent who got into trouble in the United States for his dispatches about the early battles of the Civil War.

SCOTT, FRANCIS REGINALD. *Canada Today: A Study of Her National Interests and National Policy*. London, 1939.

SIEGFRIED, ANDRE. *Canada, an International Power* (trans. from the French by Doring Hemming). 2d ed., New York, 1949.

SIEGFRIED, ANDRE. *The Race Question in Canada.* London, 1907. The most illuminating book yet written about Canada. Most of its observations are still valid.

SMITH, GOLDWIN. *Canada and the Canadian Question.* London, 1891. The gloomiest book ever written about Canada. Smith believed in the union of Canada with the United States as a prelude to "the moral federation of the English-speaking peoples."

TROLLOPE, ANTHONY. *North America.* New York, 1862.

WADE, MASON. *The French Canadian Outlook: A Brief Account of the Unknown North Americans.* New York, 1946.

WOODS, NICHOLAS AUGUSTUS. *The Prince of Wales in Canada and the United States.* London, 1861. Woods was the correspondent of the *Times* who accompanied the Prince of Wales on his visit to Canada in 1860. His letters give a striking picture of colonial loyalty in this period.

VII. *Books Dealing with Individual States*

The two Surveys of Commonwealth Affairs by Hancock and Mansergh listed in Section III contain a great deal about the recent politics of the individual members of the Commonwealth. Two series have volumes on some of the Commonwealth countries: the Modern World series, edited by H. A. L. Fisher, consisting of volumes mostly first published in the 1920's and 1930's, and the United Nations series, edited by Robert Joseph Kerner, still in process of publication by the University of California Press. Some of the books

listed in this section are short histories; the rest
deal with significant topics.

BELSHAW, HORACE, ed. *New Zealand* (United
Nations Series). Berkeley, 1947.

BRADY, ALEXANDER. *Canada* (Modern World
Series). New York, 1932.

BREBNER, JOHN BARTLETT. *North Atlantic Triangle:
The Interplay of Canada, the United States and Great
Britain.* New Haven, 1949.

BROWN, GEORGE WILLIAMS, ed. *Canada* (United
Nations Series). Berkeley, 1950.

CHATTERJEE, SIR ATUL CHANDRA. *The New India.*
London, 1948.

CLARKE, FRED. *Quebec and South Africa: A Study
in Cultural Adjustment* (University of London, Institute of Education, Studies and Reports, No. 5). Oxford,
1934.

CONDLIFFE, JOHN BELL, AND AIREY, T. G. *A Short
History of New Zealand.* Christchurch, 1955.

CORRY, JAMES ALEXANDER. *Democratic Government and Politics.* 3rd ed., Toronto, 1954. A compari-
son of the working of political machinery in Canada,
Britain, and the United States.

COUPLAND, SIR REGINALD. *The Indian Problem:
Report on the Constitutional Problem in India.* London,
1944.

CRAWFORD, RAYMOND MAXWELL. *Australia.* London, 1952.

CREIGHTON, DONALD GRANT. *Dominion of the
North: A History of Canada.* Boston, 1944.

CURTIS, EDMUND. *A History of Ireland.* 6th ed.,
London, 1950.

DAWSON, ROBERT MACGREGOR. *The Government
of Canada.* 2d ed. rev., Toronto, 1944.

FEILING, KEITH GRAHAME. *A History of England, From the Coming of the English to 1918.* London, 1950.

FITZPATRICK, BRIAN. *The Australian People, 1788-1945.* 2d ed., Melbourne, 1951.

FRANKS, SIR OLIVER SHEWELL. *Britain and the Tide of World Affairs.* London, 1955.

GARNETT, ARTHUR CAMPBELL. *Freedom and Planning in Australia.* Madison, 1949.

GLAZEBROOK, GEORGE PARKIN DE TWENEBROKER. *A History of Canadian External Relations.* Toronto, 1950.

GLEDHILL, ALAN. *The Republic of India: The Development of its Laws and Constitution.* London, 1951.

GRATTAN, CLINTON HARTLEY, ed. *Australia* (United Nations Series). Berkeley, 1947.

GRIFFITHS, SIR PERCIVAL JOSEPH. *The British Impact on India.* London, 1952.

GWYNN, STEPHEN LUCIUS. *Ireland* (Modern World Series). London, 1924.

HANCOCK, SIR WILLIAM KEITH. *Australia* (Modern World Series). 2d ed., London, 1945.

HENRY, ROBERT MITCHELL. *The Evolution of Sinn Fein.* Dublin, 1920.

HOFMEYR, JAN HENDRIK. *South Africa* (Modern World Series). 2d ed. revised and edited by J. P. Cope, London, 1952.

JENNINGS, SIR WILLIAM IVOR. *The British Constitution.* 3rd ed., Cambridge, 1950.

JENNINGS, SIR WILLIAM IVOR. *Cabinet Government.* 2d ed., Cambridge, 1951.

JENNINGS, SIR WILLIAM IVOR. *Parliament.* Cambridge, 1940.

KEITH, ARTHUR BERRIEDALE. *The Constitutional History of India, 1600-1935.* London, 1936.

KEPPEL-JONES, ARTHUR. *South Africa: A Short History.* London, 1949.

KIEWIET, CORNELIUS WILLIAM DE. *A History of South Africa, Social and Economic.* Oxford, 1941.

LEWIS, ROY, AND MAUDE, ANGUS. *The English Middle Classes.* London, 1949.

LIPSON, LESLIE. *The Politics of Equality: New Zealand's Adventures in Democracy.* Chicago, 1948.

LOWER, ARTHUR REGINALD MARSDEN. *Colony to Nation: History of Canada.* Toronto, 1946.

LYONS, FRANCIS STEWART LELAND. *The Irish Parliamentary Party, 1890-1910.* London, 1951.

McKENZIE, ROBERT TRELFORD. *British Political Parties: The Distribution of Power within the Conservative and Labour Parties.* London, 1955.

MANSERGH, NICHOLAS. *Ireland in the Age of Reform and Revolution: A Commentary on Anglo-Irish Relations and on Political Forces in Ireland, 1840-1921.* London, 1940.

MANSERGH, NICHOLAS. *The Irish Free State, Its Government and Politics.* London, 1934.

MARQUARD, LEOPOLD. *The Peoples and Policies of South Africa.* London, 1952.

MORRELL, WILLIAM PARKER. *New Zealand* (Modern World Series). London, 1935.

MOWAT, CHARLES LOCH. *Britain between the Wars, 1918-1940.* London, 1955.

O'HEGARTY, PATRICK SARSFIELD. *A History of Ireland under the Union, 1801-1920* (with an epilogue carrying the story down to the acceptance in 1927 by de Valera of the Anglo-Irish treaty of 1921). London, 1952.

OVERACKER, LOUISE. *The Australian Party System.* New Haven, 1952.

PANIKKAR, KAVALAM MADHAVA. *Asia and Western Dominance: A Survey of the Vasco da Gama Epoch of Asian History, 1498-1945.* London, 1953.

PARKIN, GEORGE RALEIGH. *India Today: An Introduction to Indian Politics.* Rev. ed., Toronto, 1946.

SHANN, EDWARD OWEN GIBLIN. *An Economic History of Australia.* Cambridge, 1930.

SPEAR, THOMAS GEORGE PERCIVAL. *India, Pakistan and the West* (Home University Library). 2d ed., London, 1952.

SPENDER, JOHN ALFRED. *Great Britain: Empire and Commonwealth, 1886-1935.* London, 1936.

STOUT, HIRAM MILLER. *British Government.* London, 1952.

THOMPSON, EDWARD JOHN, AND GARRATT, G. T. *Rise and Fulfilment of British Rule in India.* London, 1934.

TREVELYAN, GEORGE MACAULAY. *British History in the Nineteenth Century and After, 1782-1919.* London, 1947.

WADE, MASON. *The French Canadians, 1760-1945.* Toronto, 1955.

WALKER, ERIC ANDERSON. *A History of South Africa.* 2d ed., London, 1940.

WINT, GUY. *The British in Asia.* London, 1954.

WOODRUFF, PHILIP, pseud. (MASON, PHILIP). *The Men Who Ruled India.* 2 vols. London, 1954.

VIII. *Some Recent Articles and Lectures*

AMERY, JULIAN. "A Conservative View of the Commonwealth," *Political Quarterly,* XXIV (April, 1953), 167-80.

BRADY, ALEXANDER. "Nationalism and Democracy in the British Commonwealth; Some General Trends," *American Political Science Review,* XLVII (Dec., 1953), 1029-40. This and the papers by K. C. Wheare and H. Duncan Hall listed below were given at a symposium on the Commonwealth at the annual meeting of the American Political Science Association, 1953.

CARRINGTON, CHARLES EDMUND. "A New Theory of the Commonwealth," *International Affairs,* XXXI (April, 1955), 137-48.

COPLAND, SIR DOUGLAS. "The Commonwealth of Nations as a Living Organism," *South Atlantic Quarterly*, LIV (Oct., 1955), 443-52.

"The Coronation and the Commonwealth," *Round Table*, XLII (Sept., 1952), 297-304; XLIII (Dec., 1952), 3-8; (Sept., 1953), 306-15; XLIV (Dec., 1954), 57-64.

GELBER, LIONEL. "The Commonwealth and World Order," *Virginia Quarterly Review*, XXX (Winter, 1954), 6-24.

HALL, HESSEL DUNCAN. "The British Commonwealth of Nations," *American Political Science Review*, XLVII (Dec., 1953), 997-1015.

HUIZINGA, JAKOB HERMAN. "The Cult of the Commonwealth: 1. Myth or Realty? 2. From *Cives Britannica* to *Fideles Britannici*," *The Fortnightly*, CLXXIV (October, 1950), 213-19; (November, 1950), 307-11.

JENNINGS, SIR WILLIAM IVOR. "Commonwealth and Government" (two talks over the B.B.C.), *The Listener*, February 10 and 17, 1955.

JENNINGS, SIR WILLIAM IVOR. "Self Government in the Commonwealth" (eight talks over the B.B.C.), *The Listener*, July 14, 21, 28, August 4, 11, 18, 25, September 1, 1955.

McNAUGHT, KENNETH. "Ottawa and Washington Look at the United Nations," *Foreign Affairs*, XXXIII (July, 1955), 663-78.

McWHINNEY, EDWARD. "Sovereignty in the United Kingdom and the Commonwealth Countries at the Present Day," *Political Science Quarterly*, LXVIII (December, 1953), 511-25.

MANSERGH, NICHOLAS. *The Name and Nature of the British Commonwealth: An Inaugural Lecture.* Cambridge, 1954.

"Nationalism and the British Commonwealth" (five talks over the B.B.C. in 1954, published in *The Listener:*

Vincent Harlow, December 2, "The National Challenge to the Commonwealth"; Nicholas Mansergh, December 9, "The Impact of Asian Membership"; Ronald E. Robinson, December 16, "The Racial Problem in Africa"; Kenneth Robinson, December 23, "A Plea for Experiment in the Commonwealth"; Margery Perham, December 30, "Britain's Response to the End of Colonialism."

"The Nature of the Commonwealth: Is the Liberal Theory Obsolescent?" *Round Table,* XLIV (December, 1954), 9-14.

STACE, WALTER TERRENCE. "British Colonialism," *Yale Review,* XLIII (Summer, 1954), 372-84.

TAYLOR, KENNETH WIFFIN, AND CORRY, JAMES CLINTON. *Canada, the North Atlantic Community and NATO* (Royal Society of Canada pamphlets). Toronto, 1952.

WHEARE, KENNETH CLINTON. "The Nature and Structure of the Commonwealth," *American Political Science Review,* XLVII (Dec., 1953), 1016-28.

INDEX

Curtis, Lionel, and defeat of Imperial Federation, 42-47; mentioned, 19 n. 10

Defense, and Responsible Government in British colonies, 22-23; Canadian-U. S., 96-97. *See also* War
Democracy and Reaction (Hobhouse), 18
Dependencies, British, as potential members of Commonwealth, xvi-xvii
de Valera, Eamon, 48, 75
Disraeli, Benjamin, 15 and n. 7
Dominion status, 51, 74, 75, 76
Dominions, autonomy of, 47, 51-54, 56-58, 78-79
Dufferin, Lord, 27-28
Duke University Commonwealth-Studies Center, iii-v
Durham, Lord, mission to Canada, 8-9; liberalism of, 12-13; concept of a future Canadian nationality, 24-25. *See also* Durham Report
Durham Report, Responsible Government proposed in, 7-8, 18-19; four reservations, 20-23; mentioned, xxii, 66
Dyarchy, 19 and n. 10

Elizabeth II, Queen of England, 80-81, 82
Emigration, 20
Empire. *See* British Empire
Empire, The (G. Smith), 13-14
Empire-Commonwealth. *See under* British Empire
England. *See* Great Britain
English language, in India and Pakistan, 88

Federation. *See* Imperial Federation
First British Commonwealth, defined, xx-xxi; background, 30-48; Borden-Smuts Commonwealth, 49-55; King-Hertzog Commonwealth, 55-64
Franks, Sir Oliver, 72-73, 91-92
Free trade, 11-12, 12-13, 16-17, 21, 40
French Canadians, participation in Canadian government, 25-26

Gandhi, Mahatma, 78
Gelber, Lionel, xx n. 2
Gladstone, William Ewart, 74
Great Britain, and the Commonwealth, 57-58, 66, 89-90, 92-95; and Ireland, 74-76; and India, 76-80, 85, 88, 90; future of, 91-92, 94-95; and the North Atlantic triangle, 89-101 *passim*; economy of, 93, 94. *See also* British Commonwealth *and* British Empire

Hamilton, Alexander, 43
Hertzog, J. B. M., King-Hertzog Commonwealth, 55-64; and World War II, 67; mentioned, 48
High Commissioners, role in Commonwealth relations, 37-38; mentioned, 72
Hobhouse, Leonard Trelawney, 18 n. 9
Hobson, John Atkinson, 18

Imperial Conferences, and defense, 23; nature of, 36-37; federation defeated at 1911